MW01193834

Quiet Power Strategy

Tara Gentile

To Lola

"Things are only impossible until they're not."

— Jean-Luc Picard
Star Trek: The Next Generation

CONTENTS

INTRODUCTION

I work with smart, capable, creative people every day. They're doctors, academics, therapists, MBAs, coaches, and graduates of the school of life. They are wildly devoted to the work they do and the ideas they champion. Yet that drive isn't always enough to ship the products and services that will transform their customers. Their inspiration isn't always enough to build the kind of audience that will satisfy them. What makes one smart, capable, creative person incredibly productive and successful and leaves another stuck in the weeds, never realizing her full potential? The difference is self-leadership: the ability to perceive the world around her, discern the best next step, focus on the mission at hand, and, piece by piece, create a representation of her passion that feels relevant and urgent to the people who need it most.

The goal of my work is to help creative, entrepreneurial people uncover their natural self-leadership skills. This isn't a touchy-feely approach to personal development, but an identity-shifting process that leads them to see themselves as CEOs of their own ventures. The truth is that we're all Commanders-in-Chief of our own ideas, initiatives, and plans. No one is responsible for giving you the direction you need to make the choices that fulfill your mission. You need strong self-leadership to turn ideas into reality, push through discomfort, and stop at nothing to realize your goal.

When you lead yourself, you make bold choices. In order to make the best choices for yourself and your business, you need a strategy. Your Quiet Power Strategy is the roadmap for making those bold choices, leading yourself, and fulfilling your mission as only you and your business can. Whenever you're tempted to follow someone else's lead or appropriate someone else's choices, Quiet Power Strategy is the guidepost that keeps you true to what makes you most effective and compelling. It's a strategic, personal approach to leveraging what's unique about you and your business in a framework that gives you the tools you need to spend more time and energy engaging your highest value.

But before I tell you more about Quiet Power Strategy, allow me to shed light on why this concept is so important to me.

All my life, I've harbored aspirations of being everyone's favorite professor. The ivory tower called to me. I started to answer the call when I applied to graduate school in religious studies. I was accepted at my top-choice school. I received a full tuition scholarship. I was to study with my hero. (Yes, even theologians can be heroes.)

And then I bailed. The path in front of me felt more like a road to nowhere than a path to satisfaction. There was no guarantee I would complete my PhD, no assurance that I would land a professorship if I did receive my degree, and no promise that a professorship would offer much in the way of financial security if I did get one. I decided to trade uncertainty for a steady paycheck. Even still, I was just trading one set of choices for another set of choices. I was 21, and none of those choices were really my own. I was just trying on different hats to see which fit.

When I shared the news with my advisor, I sat in his living room and wept. I avoided contact with my friends and mentors because of the shame I felt about veering from the path. I spent most of my twenties feeling like an unredeemable failure.

In those years, I daydreamed about getting back to the classroom. I researched programs, thought about new fields of study, and printed out countless applications. But in all that time, I never sent one. Despite being a smart, creative, capable person, I couldn't get this simple task done. Instead, I continued to work in retail management, enjoying my job in theory but hating how there were never enough resources to accomplish our goals, how I worked long hours with little thanks, and how I returned home every day emotionally drained. In my fifth year with the company, I had the opportunity to interview for the top position at my store. I had been training and preparing for this for years and had been ensured I was a shoo-in for the job.

I interviewed, 9 months pregnant, and wowed the interviewer. Two weeks later, I learned that the position was given to someone else who had less experience and less time with the company than I did. I remember the details so clearly. It was my first day of maternity leave and I was at the grocery store when the call came. I can see the stacks of Brawny I was waddling toward when my friend told me the news. I hung up the phone, my heart filled with rage, knowing two things: I needed to give myself a couple of days to process, and I was never going to work for that company again.

After I processed what happened, I sat down at the dining room table with a notebook and pen. I wrote down all the skills I had that could be of use to organizations. Then I wrote down all the organizations I wanted to offer those skills to. I had decided that if other people could work from home, so could I. And, I was going to do it based on what I wanted to offer, how I wanted to work, and who I wanted to work with. That notebook contained my very first Quiet Power strategic plan.

That plan never really came to fruition. Instead, over 5 years after quitting the academic track and 5 months after getting passed over for the promotion, my mom called me with an idea for a website. I bought the domain name immediately after getting off the phone. I had the site built days later, I gathered a community, and I started sharing stories daily on January 2, 2009. The birth of that site led to countless opportunities and has evolved into a venture that can only be described as exactly what I imagined in my wildest dreams.

I struggled to send in the graduate school applications or see a future in a company where my talents weren't recognized because I hadn't yet realized that my future depended on me being able to lead myself, take agency over my livelihood, and create the life and career in which I could be most effective. It required a strong focus on the vision of what I wanted to create, the perception to seize opportunities in front of me, and the discernment of how I wanted to connect with others. The life I have now, and the career I continue to hone, are a direct reflection of this focus, perception, and discernment. I live my Quiet Power Strategy every day, and I lead myself to create and connect in the way I want in order to fulfill my personal mission.

Maybe you, too, have had the frustration of not being able to make things happen the way you think they should. You just can't get traction. You don't, or won't, complete things that should be easy to complete. What action you do take only makes you feel more and more lost or ineffective. That's when you need your own Quiet Power Strategy.

The career and business I have now is truly based on what makes me most effective. I waste little time on all the noise of the market; instead, I focus only on what's going to get me closer to my goals. The good news is that this is not a superpower reserved for a select few but a strategic approach that you can craft for yourself. You can learn to edit out the "shoulds" and focus on doing only those things that are getting you closer to where you want to go. This is not just a personal approach to life but a personalized approach to business. You can build a whole venture around your Quiet Power Strategy and invite those who complement your strategic plan to join you, create with you, and buoy you.

Your Quiet Power Strategy comes down to choices. There are very few "musts" in the world of business. When you decide what you want to create and how you want to connect with others to provide that value, you make proactive decisions that form a plan that's uniquely yours.

You could try to follow everyone else's lead. You could try to squeeze your business into someone else's plan, or use someone else's strategy. But in the end, it won't work. They're not you. You're not me.

I'm the woman who overthinks just about everything except when to start. I'm the geek that loves Star Trek and Doctor Who. I'm the fan who has listened to the audiobook of Tina Fey's Bossypants at least a hundred times (no joke). And I'm the beer snob who is pretentious about it even though I only started drinking beer about 18 months ago.

This is just who I am; it's all part of my unique personal makeup. These are the things that inform the choices I make about what I want to create and how I want to connect with others. These are the things that attract people to my business. These are the things that make me more powerful. These are the things that help me push the edges of my own work and look for opportunities where there were none. Being clear and comfortable with what makes me me leads to more proactive decisions about how I lead my business.

Using my own unique choices, I've built a bigger business than I could have ever imagined when I first decided to create work for myself. My reputation often feels larger than life. And yet, I haven't done a lot of things people say you have to do when you're building a business. Most importantly, I haven't done what doesn't feel true to my sense of leadership or my unique set of skills, strengths, and passions.

When you think of power, you might envision monarchies or moguls, but there's an everyday power that truly influential people and businesses use to inspire, motivate, and challenge their communities. That's the kind of power I use in my business and the kind of power my business is known for. My business has a reputation for pushing our clients to bigger and better places, advocating for ideas that are new to the market, and considering fresh ways to do business within our sphere of influence.

As I leaned in to the quiet power in my business, I noticed others doing something similar for themselves. These quietly powerful business owners were focused on making their businesses uniquely attractive, being true to their core strengths, and being unapologetic about their own proclivities and priorities.

These entrepreneurs might not be helming the businesses everyone is talking about, but they lead businesses that have loyal communities that refer new customers and help make better products. These entrepreneurs have discovered the business models, marketing campaigns, sales processes, and internal systems that allow them to thrive with ease. They've leveraged their own self-leadership to create more, connect more, and succeed more than others.

I began looking for the themes of how these businesses were run—their strategic approach—and found many things in common. The principles were applied differently but, in essence, were the same.

It was the approach these businesses shared that I started calling Quiet Power Strategy.

You can find Quiet Power Strategy at work in all aspects of life and in all markets. You'll recognize those people and brands not by what they say about themselves but how they show up, what they do, and where they lead themselves. You'll see their devoted fans sharing their ads, snatching up new products, and cheering on employees. These entrepreneurs might fly under the radar for a time, but eventually others catch on to their innate authenticity and inherent power.

Crafting Your Own Quiet Power Strategy

As you go through this book, and as you begin to craft your own Quiet Power Strategy, it will be essential to consider a set of core strategic questions. We'll examine them at length later. For now, consider your gut reaction to each:

- What is your vision for making life meaningfully better for your audience, clients, or customers and how will you measure your success?
- What conversation is your business a part of and what voices in that conversation are your best prospects looking for an alternative to?
- What will you use to represent your unique point of view to engage customers who are excited about your business's strengths, skills, and passion?
- How will you further invest in your unique point of view to attract your best prospects?
- What product, marketing, sales, and management systems can you put in place to support and enhance your business's unique point of view?

In Chapter 1, you'll learn more about what Quiet Power Strategy is, who it's for, and who is already using it. You'll discover that Quiet Power isn't just for introverts, and it's not about playing small.

In Chapter 2, I explain why self-leadership is so important for the noisy world we find ourselves living in. Creatives often encounter the same roadblocks to accessing their self-leadership skills; I'll explain what they are and how to look out for those on your own path.

Chapter 3 guides you through answering the 5 core questions (listed above) that you need to address to create a strategic approach to your business today. These questions are based on this new economic period called the Social Era.

Chapters 4, 5, and 6 center on the core skills you need for acting on your Quiet Power Strategy: perception, discernment, and focus. I'll show you how business owners today are using these skills to find success that's uniquely their own.

In Chapter 7, I'll show you how to hone your personal approach to your business and help you create your Quiet Power Strategic Plan. You'll find the key components of creating your Quiet Power Strategy plus exercises that will guide you to discovering your business's strategic direction. Then, you can lead yourself on the course of action that will make your business most effective.

The final section of the book provides the Quiet Power Strategy prompts. These prompts act as creative triggers to help you see past conventional thinking or ingrained patterns and get back to what makes you most unique and effective so you can use that to guide your business.

In the end, I hope you choose to lead yourself to the wealth, peace, and ease you crave. I hope you choose to lead your business and your community to the power that comes from keen perception, careful discernment, and clear focus. Quiet Power Strategy is a great way to do just that.

PART ONE:
QUIET POWER

Chapter 1

What Is Quiet Power Strategy?

Your Quiet Power Strategy is your personal approach to what works. It's perceiving, discerning, and focusing on what is going to create the greatest opportunity for service while allowing you to leverage both how you work best and what you want most. It's not "quiet" as in library quiet. It's "quiet" as in that still, small voice that lives inside each of us.

You can be bold, boisterous, or bawdy and still leverage Quiet Power Strategy.

You see, the opposite of Quiet isn't Loud; it's Noise. We live in a world full of Noise: media, gurus, and hot new things. Too often, we search for answers in the Noise. We look for direction. We look for Power. You won't find Power in the Noise. You find Power in the Quiet. You discover what is powerful about you and your business only when you create the Quiet for yourself.

At its core, Quiet Power Strategy asks you to focus on what you are driven to create and how you best connect with the people who will be served by that creation. This is the Social Era and you are a brand; whether you're dealing with a relationship, a career, or a strategic plan for multimillion-dollar growth, Quiet Power Strategy applies. For the purpose of this book, we'll be focusing on business, but the insights you discover about your own Quiet Power will resonate across all aspects of your life.

Your Quiet Power Strategy gives direction to your business, creates peace and ease, and, perhaps most importantly, helps your business stand out in a Noisy world. Traditional business strategy focused on creating competitive advantage, which assumes a zero-sum game where there are winners and losers. In contrast, Quiet Power Strategy helps you find your "generative advantage." Umair Haque, a Thinkers50 thought leader and consultant, asserts that generative advantage is more in keeping with the next evolution of capitalism. When you create your generative advantage in the market, you're creating more authentic value and wealth. Instead of taking a bigger piece of the pie, you're baking a bigger pie.

Your strategy should focus on how your business can create something new, not just get a piece of what already exists. By doing that, and by basing your creation on your own unique makeup, your business will stand out in our Noisy world.

Why Should You Care?

Squeezing your business (or career, or relationship, or lifestyle) into someone else's plan hurts, and it denies your own self-leadership. Trying to follow someone else's lead leaves you flailing and frustrated. It's not the good kind of discomfort that comes from pushing edges that need to be pushed to see growth. It's disease.

We often ignore the difference between dis-comfort and dis-ease in the course of either pushing ourselves to be something we're not or beating ourselves up for not being good enough, motivated enough, or strong enough. Dis-comfort will come from discovering what it is about you and your business that really works and pushing that to the nth degree. Dis-ease will come from feeling like you're constantly teetering on the edge of a cliff. On the other side of discomfort, there's growth. On the other side of dis-ease is a long, fast fall.

Maybe you've been teetering on that edge for too long, maybe you've been beating yourself up about not pushing harder, or maybe you're just confused about why everything you try just doesn't seem to catch fire like it has for others.

Wherever you find yourself, you're not alone.

Beginning to claim your own Quiet Power can help. Quiet Power Strategy begins by recognizing the connection between what is out there (perception) and what is true for you (discernment). Then, it manifests by taking action that makes that connection stronger, more meaningful, and more real (focus). Instead of a mess of tactics that don't relate particularly well to your understanding of the world around you or the truth of what you know about yourself, you have the clarity of a strategy that is particular to you and your business.

If you've ever struggled to get traction with your business, Quiet Power Strategy is for you. Traction is born from authenticity, alignment, and truth. It happens when people recognize that unique connection that you've forged between yourself and the world around you—including them. It's that spark of recognition that causes marketing campaigns to ignite or brands to become communities.

And what's more, it's easy.

"Struggle" isn't a word that should be synonymous with business. The key to finding more ease in your business is to make product development, marketing, business models, sales processes, and growth all grounded in your unique makeup and what it brings to your business. Your skills, passions, point of view, quirks, and modus operandi form the basis for developing a unique business strategy that, by its very nature, will incorporate more ease into your business.

Your personal values and guiding principles shape the decision-making and vision-crafting in your business so each action you take aligns with what brings you ease.

The more you can tap into the truth these questions reveal, the easier it is to gain traction, build a platform, and boost sales—in short, the easier it is to lead yourself where you want to go.

Quiet Power Strategy helps you access the personal truth you need to leverage to make your business successful. By defining the path of your business based on your unique point of view, What You Want to Create, and How You Want to Connect, the course will be much easier to navigate. Instead of trying to make others' strategies work for you, you focus first on what works for you and then create a strategy that matches.

Who Uses Quiet Power Strategy?

Let's start with who doesn't use Quiet Power Strategy. There are reality TV stars, for one. You might also include hedge fund managers. (The ones I've known who are drawn to Quiet Power Strategy have gotten out of the hedge funds and into creating more holistic wealth management for clients.) There are also many politicians, the kind that check which way the wind is blowing before they open their mouths, to make sure what they say is riding the right trend.

It's not that any of these people are bad people, per se. It's that they aren't leveraging the power they already possess. They're not intentional about what they're creating or how they're connecting with others. They're working a plan that's been given to them and using the Noise to their advantage. They're leveraging the power of voyeur television or regulatory loopholes or their constituents' fears. It works. But it won't work forever.

When you try to squeeze yourself or your business into

someone else's plan, you have to work the Noise to get attention. You contribute to the overwhelm instead of trying to create peace. You do all the things that, while they could be perfectly aligned for someone else, just feel off to you. Every day, you end up feeling forced into that insistent, almost desperate, action that comes from clinging to someone else's understanding of what works. That unyielding push to manifest success on someone else's terms and with someone else's plan isn't effective, and it isn't attractive.

Adding to the Noise isn't a good strategy because it's based on structures that are inherently ephemeral. At best, Noisy works for a short period of time. Then the rules change and you have to adapt your act. In a world where the rules are constantly changing, it's much easier to tap into what you and others value about you so you can lead yourself.

It seems hard to find models of Quiet Power Strategy success, mostly because those people and businesses are busy doing their thing and making stuff happen. So we don't consciously think, "Oh, there's someone who has it figured out" or "There's a plan I can use."

But people who leverage Quiet Power Strategy are all around us: Oprah, Tina Fey, Richard Branson, Jimmy Fallon, Adele, Cheryl Strayed, Elizabeth Gilbert, J. K. Rowling, David Sedaris, Neil deGrasse Tyson. These are people who play the game, but on their own terms. They've decided what rules they'll follow and which they'll break. They've decided that, if they can't build exactly what they want, they won't build it.

Speaking of Tina Fey, I think it's high time for a Tina Fey quote: "Don't waste your energy trying to educate or change opinions; go over, under, through, and opinions will change organically when you're the boss. Or they won't. Who cares? Do your thing, and don't care if they like it."

The key here is that when you do your thing, when you make your magic, it doesn't matter if everybody likes it, because you doing your thing is more attractive to the right people. You do, however, need to make adjustments, optimize, and create leverage when you're doing your own thing. That's what I hear when Fey says "go over, under, through."

That's what Quiet Power Strategy is all about. It's a strategic approach to doing things your way. It's the process of discovery and insight that allows you to "go over, under, through" the formulas and best practices keeping you and your business from financial, personal, and creative fulfillment.

Is Quiet Power Strategy Just for Introverts?

Quiet Power Strategy is not just for introverts. Quiet Power Strategy isn't about being shy, introverted, or timid. It's not about internal processing, hedging, or what's energetically draining.

Quiet Power Strategy is about your sense of self-leadership and the choices you make as a business owner. When you prioritize what you do best, most powerfully, and most valuably, people take notice. You become known as a leader. Your brand is perceived as more powerful. Your offers and invitations are more readily accepted. You don't have to hustle or add to the Noise to create the perception of status; you embody status. And that's possible for introverts and extroverts alike.

I know many extroverts who embody Quiet Power Strategy. And I know many introverts who struggle trying to keep up with the Noise. Over the course of this book, I'll pose questions that you can use to discover your own Quiet Power and apply it to a strategy for personal and business success no matter who you are or how personality tests may label you.

Why Is This More Relevant Now Than Ever Before?

We are all making our own way now. We're co-creating a new economy where careers are things made by individuals, not corporations. We're taking agency over our livelihoods. We're recognizing what makes each of us a valuable part of the team. We're working in niche markets and finding scale in smaller communities. If this isn't the time to dig in to what makes you or your business unique, I don't know what is.

The New Economy is about creation and connection. To approach your business strategically in the New Economy, you need to know what you're going to create and how to connect with the people who will respond to it. The New Economy is business made personal. That's why your personal strategy and business strategy are simply two sides of the same coin.

Quiet Power Strategy sets you up for lasting success in this new frontier of entrepreneurship.

Chapter 2

Self-Leadership, Creatives, And The New Economy

Want to sell the products you design or offer your expertise for a price? You don't need to get anyone's permission today. You don't need a bank loan, you don't need a storefront, and you certainly don't need a degree or seal of approval. You can buy a domain name, sign up for a service like Shopify or Squarespace, and start selling in minutes. You can release a movie or publish a book without a production company or a publishing house. The possibilities are truly endless. But because there are fewer gatekeepers, permission-givers, and clear paths to success than at any other time in history, you can't rely on anyone else to tap you on the shoulder and say, "Step forward. This is your time."

If you won't do it for yourself, no one is going to do it for you.

When the possibilities are endless, the options can be overwhelming. While there are fewer gatekeepers and permission-givers, there are many more ways to create your own livelihood. There is almost an infinite number of ways to take your idea to market, communicate with the people who need it most, and partner with others to reach your goals. And, there is an almost infinite number of best practices espoused by consultants, authors, and bloggers.

Infinite choices and possibilities are overwhelming. Self-leadership is your path out of the overwhelm. If you aren't leading yourself, it doesn't mean the possibilities and opportunities aren't there; it means that you have difficulty making meaningful progress toward your goals because you can't navigate all the options. When you're not tapped in to your self-leadership, you feel like you're lacking a clear sense of direction, and you don't have the intense focus that enables you to prioritize action and production to create your vision.

The problem is that self-leadership doesn't come naturally and, even when it does, it's beaten out of us at an early age. It's not something that is taught in schools or encouraged in the workplace. Instead instead of learning how to guide ourselves, we learn how to comply with the system and play the game within the rules.

So even if you were,you may as you go looking for the gatekeeper, leader, or manager that you've been taught to please. Now that you're in charge, you have to train yourself to look within and find the answers you're seeking. Self-leadership is the key to creating a framework that has you relying more on yourself than on gurus or can't-lose formulas.

Self-leadership isn't about being more productive; it's about being more effective. You don't have to do or produce more. Instead, you need to make what you're doing or producing really count. The best way to do that is to work what's true for you and how you really want to connect with people into everything you do. Position your work in a way that's aligned with the way you show up naturally, and you'll find traction and effectiveness less fleeting.

To better lead yourself, you need to hone 3 key skills: perception, discernment, and focus. In the old economy, most of us outsourced these skills. We relied on others to tell us what was going on in our world, we sought plans and formulas from people who knew better than us, and we waited for management to tell us what to put our attention on.

Today, there are both fewer ways to outsource these skills and many more opportunities to take control for yourself. But now that you have control, what are you going to do with it? You can control yourself into a hole in the ground or you can lead yourself where you want to go. You can get bogged down in busywork or you can devise creative plans and watch them work. You can force yourself to struggle through the conventional way or decide to blaze your own path.

Perception, discernment, and focus will help you find your own way. When you hone your perception, you see, hear, feel, and sense more of what is going on around you. You have more information to work with. You feel better prepared and more out in front of the market. When you refine your skill of discernment, you use the information at your disposal to get closer to your own goals. You see opportunities for creativity instead of either/or choices. When you sharpen your focus, you only spend time doing work that counts. You know what's going to push the needle and you concentrate on those things.

Using these skills, you can rely less on outside direction and more on your own self-leadership. You can take advantage of all the opportunities the New Economy affords you without getting stuck in the weeds. Tapping into your own self-leadership makes you more powerful, quietly. When you're more effective, more focused, more perceptive and aligned with the market, you exude authority. When you're leading yourself, others want to follow you.

If you're in the position of needing to convince others to trust you, to cultivate a sense of community and belonging, and to present yourself as powerful—and we all are—invest yourself in becoming a keen self-leader.

Creative people like us face many roadblocks on the path to realizing our full potential and self-leadership. The obvious roadblocks are things like too many ideas, perfectionism, and lack of support. But there are many more insidious reasons people don't end up where they want to be each year. These reasons are dangerous because they often seem like common sense, but it's really fear and discomfort masquerading as the voice of wisdom.

The first of these reasons is false assumptions. We often make assumptions because we fear challenging ourselves and looking for the truth. Assumptions seem safe, tried and true. Unfortunately, they lead us down paths that cause more heartache and hassle than taking time to seek out what's really true. In my work, I see clients battle assumptions about how much people are willing to pay for a product or service, how prospects will react to a new idea or format, or what people are willing to buy based on what's already on the market. These assumptions keep them from innovating and exploring new ideas.

Assumptions also keep people from leading themselves to new destinations. According to famed management writer Ken Blanchard, "In business and in their personal lives, many people who are having trouble accomplishing goals suffer quietly by assuming the worst. They think they don't have the power to do anything about it and refuse to ask for the help they need. Effective self-leaders are able to avoid self-defeating beliefs, leverage their points of power, and collaborate with others—resulting in goal achievement, independence, and the ability to lead others more effectively." People with strong self-leadership skills avoid assuming the worst when things don't go their way. Instead, they seek a new understanding of the world around them and use their own personal strengths to make connections with this new perspective.

Instead of believing the worst about everything that stands in your way, look for contrary information. In the digital age, we're especially prone to only exposing ourselves to media and data that confirm our assumptions. If you find yourself susceptible to making assumptions about what is and isn't possible, make a list of all the roadblocks standing between you and your goal. Then research whether those things are, in fact, the truth. It can take some real digging, so don't give up easily and enlist help if you need it. That's what Stacey did.

Stacey Howe-Lott is an SAT coach and the founder of Stellar Scores. She primarily works with students who have more going on than just test prep. She loves helping student athletes, drama kids, and aspiring musicians get significantly better test scores so they can get acceptance letters to their top-choice schools without devoting all of their time to studying. When Stacey came to me, she was working through a lot of assumptions. The first assumption she made was that she had to work with students one-on-one to help them create personalized plans. The second assumption was that she couldn't raise her hourly rate because she was already at the top of the market. In other words, her assumptions had her stuck. Yet she believed there was a better way.

During the process of finding her Quiet Power Strategy, she busted those assumptions. Stacey realized that the value she offered wasn't in working one-on-one with students but the unique coaching methodology and analytics she used to inform her tutoring plans. That meant she could scale what she was offering to work with more and more students at once. She also experimented with higher pricing and found that the results she delivered, in the time frame she delivered them, could carry prices well above top market rates. Since making these changes, Stacey's business growth has been massive. At the time I'm writing, she's on track to triple her revenue this year and has a plan to triple it again next year. Stacey is now making easeful decisions based on what's actually true instead of what she assumes.

The next roadblock creative people face before they tap into their Quiet Power Strategy is the Impostor Complex. It's that nagging voice that tells you that you're not good enough yet or that one day everyone will find out you're a fraud. It pushes you to squeeze yourself into a sure-thing plan. It compels you to search and search for a formula or strategy that originates with someone more seasoned, more experienced, or smarter than you. And when that strategy doesn't work out, you find the fault with yourself instead of the strategy.

The Impostor Complex makes you discount yourself first and foremost. But as Tanya Geisler, my life coach and an expert on the Impostor Complex, reminds us, "The very fact that you are experiencing the Impostor Complex in the first place is proof that you are conscientious, high-functioning, and have strong values of integrity and excellence." It stands to reason, then, that you might have a few good ideas about how to do things your own way based on your unique personal values, strengths, and makeup.

How do you get in touch with those good ideas and the personal sovereignty that you have trouble accessing while bogged down by Impostor Complex? Your unique personal makeup is the source of your Quiet Power Strategy and the key to finding your own way forward. You have to know yourself and your power to make your own way. Luckily, that's a lot easier than always chasing the hot new thing. Nilofer Merchant, author of 11 *Rules for Creating Value in the #SocialEra*, calls your unique makeup your Onlyness. She writes, "Onlyness is that thing that only one particular person can bring to a situation. It includes the skills, passions, and purpose of each human. Onlyness is fundamentally about honoring each person, first as we view ourselves and second as we are valued."

If you find that Impostor Complex is forcing you to constantly chase the latest-greatest formulas and discount following your own way forward, take inventory of your

Onlyness. Get clear on exactly what skills, passions, and purpose you possess. Look from your own perspective and then seek out evidence of how others perceive and value you at your best. You can weigh every idea, every piece of criticism, every tactic, and every taunt from your Impostor Complex against that inventory. Just getting that piece of the puzzle in place is a personal transformation in itself.

The third roadblock creative people face is the compulsion to fix weaknesses instead of leveraging their strengths. In every employee assessment you've ever received, you've likely been told about some "areas of opportunity." Of course, "areas of opportunity" is simply a euphemism for weaknesses. You're told that if you can improve on those things, you'll become better, smarter, faster. Following this same logic, many creative people, spend time and energy trying to "fix" themselves. However, strength psychology researchers Donald O. Clifton and Tom Rath, along with the Gallup research organization, found that "people have several times more potential for growth when they invest energy in developing their strengths instead of correcting their deficiencies."

If you've ever taken the StrengthsFinder assessment, developed by Clifton and Rath, you've received a clear look into how your strengths set you up for creating exponentially more value than you could by fixing your weaknesses. I look at my own StrengthsFinder results every day as a way of reminding myself to let go of ideas, projects, or tasks that don't play into those aspects of my unique composition. StrengthsFinder, though, is just one way to get back in touch with your core strengths.

I'm also a huge fan of the work of Sally Hogshead and her company, Fascinate, Inc. In her New York Times bestselling book *How the World Sees You*, Hogshead advocates for using the natural ways you communicate to differentiate yourself from the rest of the market and make you more compelling. When you are more fascinating and memorable to the people around you, and when your communication is naturally more effective and produces results more often, you're less likely to get caught up in your weaknesses and discount the power of your unique makeup.

The final roadblock to transformation that creatives face is difficulty admitting what's wrong or what's not working. My friend Jennifer Louden, author of The Life Organizer, wrote on Facebook the other day, "To me it seems like one of our biggest issues as humans is often our inability to look, to face into what we don't like." I immediately thought of the business owners I come in contact with on a daily basis.

While Louden was writing about a cultural issue, this parallel application in business was compounded by the fact that it was a Facebook post. Whether it's Facebook, Instagram, Pinterest, or whatever social media platform has struck your fancy, there is a documented tendency to sugar-coat what's not working and, in some way or another, make it look like it is working. We'll do anything—including cleaning one corner of the kitchen to get the perfect lunch shot—to appear like our results match our vision. And while I believe most of the people who would read this kind of book are glass-half-full kind of people, it quickly becomes frustrating and disillusioning to affect those kinds of results instead of embodying them.

Now I'm not suggesting that part of your personal transformation into Quiet Power should be airing your dirty laundry on every social media platform you frequent. Not hardly. What I am suggesting is that being honest with yourself about what is and what isn't working is a key part of creating a strategic plan for getting where you want to go. When you acknowledge what's not working, you can take time to objectively judge whether those things are even necessary.

Dr. Samantha Brody—my friend, client, and doctor—told me in our very first strategy session that she often asks patients, "How is that working for you?" after they detail their health routines. Getting 5 hours of sleep a night? How's that working for you? Drinking 5 cups of coffee after lunch? How's that working for you? Sitting behind a desk for 10 hours straight? How's that working for you?

I often ask my clients the very same thing. Sometimes, the answer is "It works great!" and, while their tactic might be unconventional, I leave it alone. Other times, the answer is "It kind of sucks..." and we look for a better way. Just as fixing your weaknesses isn't always the answer, the solution here isn't always to optimize the root behavior, routine, or tactic. Many times, it's to find a new behavior, routine, or tactic that will work better based on the unique composition of the person, not convention.

Acknowledging what's not working isn't the same as acknowledging that you'd be better off doing what you "should" have been doing from the beginning. On the contrary, it's the first step to figuring out what will be uniquely effective for you, regardless of all the "shoulds" and "supposed tos." It's like Tina Fey says in Bossypants: "When people say, 'You really, really must' do something, it means you don't really have to. No one ever says, 'You really, really must deliver the baby during labor.' When it's true, it doesn't need to be said." Sure, there are things you must do in business, namely have a product or service to sell. But most of the "shoulds" are negotiable. If there's something you think your business should do but it doesn't line up with What You Want to Create or How You Want to Connect with your customers5, try something else.

I'm sure these roadblocks to success and business growth sound familiar: succumbing to false assumptions, following other people's plans instead of your own, fixing your weaknesses instead of doubling down on your strengths, and ignoring what's not working. The good news, of course, is that there is a strategic plan and corresponding actions you can take so that you don't get stuck when you reach one of these roadblocks. You can find your way over, under, or through it. There is a better way to get where you're going: yours.

Chapter 3

5 Key Questions for Uncovering Your Quiet Power Strategy

You can know all the latest and greatest tactics in your industry. You can have your finger on the pulse of what's hot in your field. But if you don't have a clear picture of your overall strategy for business, those tactics are worthless. What's more, if your business strategy isn't grounded in a keen knowledge of the people you want to connect with and the ideas you want to realize through your products, services, or offers, you'll be constantly in the weeds and never making real progress toward your goals.

Understanding your Quiet Power Strategy is the first step to setting your business up for success. When you know what you want and what works most naturally for you, you can put the hot tactics and trends to use—and better yet, start to develop some of your own. You can effectively lead yourself and your team to achieve individual metrics and incremental goals. You'll finish every day feeling more productive, further along, and more aligned with your vision.

Roger Martin, author of Playing to Win, defines business strategy as "an integrated set of choices that uniquely positions the firm in its industry so as to create sustainable advantage and superior value relative to the competition." He emphasizes that strategy is about the choices we make in the course of creating a plan for business. I couldn't agree more. When you're struggling to get ahead, it can feel like there are certain things you have to do. The non-negotiables start stacking up and your own wisdom and self-leadership get drowned out in the Noise. But everything in business is a choice, and the choices you make determine your strategy. When you're conscious and in control of those choices, you can construct a strategy that will make your vision a reality.

Martin goes on to outline 5 questions that are key to understanding the choices available to you as a business owner or manager while determining your strategy. I appreciate his more traditional approach and the language he uses around playing to win; however, I believe an updated approach is more helpful for New Economy entrepreneurs in the Social Era. The essence of Martin's approach–that business is a game and that there's a clear path to winning– resonates in the business arena populated with career managers and MBAs, but it falls short of capturing the reality of the creative or idea-driven market today. Quiet Power Strategy, therefore, is an update and repurposing of some of Martin's ideas for entrepreneurs like you who are building communities and movements as much as they are building revenue streams and management systems.

Instead of Martin's terms "Where to Play" and "How to Win," it's more helpful and attuned with our Social Era to consider "What to Create" and "How to Connect." Your Quiet Power Strategy should outline what is most important to you in terms of filling out your legacy or body of work (what you're creating), what conversation you want to participate in (where you're creating), and how you'll connect with the people who need your ideas or perspective (how you're connecting). What You Want to Create and How You Want to Connect are largely dictated by how you can be most effective and what feels most natural to you. What makes you most effective is your Quiet Power.

In the introduction, I introduced 5 key questions for starting to formulate your own Quiet Power Strategy. Now it's time to learn more about how each of those questions influences your business and decision-making.

What is your vision for making life meaningfully better for your audience, clients, or customers and how will you measure your success?

To start creating a more effective strategy for your business, define your vision. Even if it seems difficult to look years—even months—in advance, you need to have an idea of what you're building. Your movement needs to take a shape, your conversation needs to take a particular direction, your product needs to have a purpose. You don't need a 5- or 10-year plan, but you must commit to at least a working definition of your vision.

The easiest way to define your vision is by focusing on how you'll make people's lives meaningfully better through what you're creating. Umair Haque writes in his book *Betterness*, "Maybe you believe that, at its best, humankind is capable of reaching not merely for the mall and the big-box store, impelled by the bonus and the corner office, but for the stars and beyond, propelled by the luminous promise of lives meaningfully better lived and the unconquered challenge of scaling the highest peaks of human potential." Your business doesn't need to be motivated by how wide you can make your profit margin or how much you can shrink expenses. Instead, you can choose to fuel your business with the positive influence you're having in people's lives and the meaning you're creating with them.

Dr. Samantha Brody, whom I mentioned earlier, is a naturopathic physician and licensed acupuncturist. She's defined her vision by focusing on helping to create health-conscious people who make more personalized, proactive decisions to feel good every day. She knows she's most effective when she helps her patients and clients identify the personal values that guide their lives and how those values can be used to guide their health choices. Really, she helps them find the Quiet Power Strategy for their health! Her patients experience positive changes in their health not by trying to do everything, but by making laser-focused adjustments based on their personal values and priorities. She wants to see a whole generation of health seekers make better health decisions on their own without following all the fads or gurus.

Knowing that, Dr. Samantha can position her services well in a very crowded market. She can easily communicate just what kind of results you can expect from working with her and how she guides you to those results differently than her competition. She can make better choices about her price point, her marketing tactics, and her sales processes.

Once you've got your vision in place, it's important to define how you'll measure your level of success in attaining your vision. Identify the specific mile markers that signify your progress. Do you need to grow your email list? Do you want to publish a book? Do you want to win an award? Throw a major event? Land a serious donation to your cause? Establishing your vision and your metrics means that your vision isn't just a dream but the start of a workable plan.

What conversation is your business a part of and what voices in that conversation are your best prospects looking for an alternative to?

"Markets are conversations." That's what the book The Cluetrain Manifesto teaches about business in the age of the internet. It seems a new app or network to facilitate conversation and personal influence launches every day. That means you and your business need to be part of the conversation if you want to succeed.

The vision you hold for your business and your community determines the overall conversation you're part of, but it's still a choice. Dr. Samantha could choose to participate in the general health conversation or she could focus on talking with entrepreneurs who are trying to maximize their health. She could focus on the wellness side of the foodie conversation or she could focus on the fitness side of the lifestyle conversation. Don't ever allow yourself to be caged into a conversation you haven't chosen to be a part of. Make a choice.

Once that choice is made, seek out the existing voices in the conversation in which you want to position your business. These are the leaders, businesses, and influencers that make up the "sound" of the market. They're the ones that have, thus far, set the tone and guided the conversation.

Your business has an opportunity to differentiate itself in part by what voices you choose to set up as an alternative to. When you do that, you can use your Quiet Power to be more effective through all areas of your marketing, outreach, and sales. There are always people actively looking for an alternative to the loudest voices. There are always people looking for a better fit for the things they want to talk about and explore. Ask yourself what voices you can provide an alternative to for the people who matter most to you (your community and prospective customers). Make a list of their names and their businesses. Then jot down what about those voices people are looking to break away from.

Think about how Steve Jobs positioned Apple after returning as CEO. He looked at the existing conversation around personal computing where more, more, and more always seemed to be the answer, and he instead presented a case for design, curation, and efficiency. Apple was an alternative that galvanized a whole segment of the market who became not only fiercely loyal customers but brand evangelists that helped to grow Apple's market share.

You don't have to demonize or reject the other influencers in the market. It's not about saying others are doing it wrong, just that you're doing it differently. Positioning yourself, your business, and your voice as an alternative to what people are used to hearing gives you an opportunity to be memorable right out of the gate. It helps you create your generative advantage and bake a bigger pie.

What will you use to represent your unique point of view to engage customers who are excited about your business's strengths, skills, and passion?

Once you know which conversation your business is a part of and you know what voices you want to position yours as an alternative to, you need to determine how you'll represent your unique voice. Look to your unique strengths, skills, and passions. Identify your obsessions, the things that get you riled up, and the things that unlock your ability to connect with others.

The more you differentiate your voice and unique point

of view based on those things, the "softer" you can speak while still making an enormous impact. Your influence becomes tied to how well you speak your own message in your own words, with your own quirks, instead of how loudly you try to echo or agree with others. Maybe this appears obvious to you. If so, ask yourself if your business has fully integrated that kind of differentiation. Whether on Main Street, in Silicon Valley, or on the internet superhighway, I hear many more voices saying "Me too!" than clearly stating their difference.

The personal development conversation is a great example of this. Anyone can read a few self-help books, change a few habits, and tell you to do the same. Anyone can repeat the same old cheers from the sidelines of life, waving tired pompoms in the air. Anyone can string together the language of the genre and tell you to live your best, most authentic, most passionate life. This is the kind of lackluster drivel that's easy to overlook and that rarely galvanizes a community.

Then someone comes along who has chosen to eschew the typical trappings of the personal development conversation and instead talk about life in terms of the scriptural narratives that affect our thought and behavior patterns, the way Ronna Detrick, author of A Feminist with Faith, does, and we sit up and take notice. Ronna isn't interested in just being another voice in the personal development choir. She's not interested in preaching the same message as other people working at the intersection of leadership and feminist narratives. Ronna uses her passion for retelling the stories we grew up with in Sunday School, as well as her background in theology and hermeneutics, to show women how to reprogram long-standing beliefs about how they should act and think.

As you craft your own Quiet Power Strategy, make sure that your business's voice focuses on what makes it unique, not how it blends in.

How will you invest in your unique point of view to attract your best prospects?

It's not enough to just know what your unique qualities and proclivities are; you need to double down on them. Highlighting, even emphasizing, them is what makes you and your business really stand out. With the advent of social media and social business, you have more tools at your disposal than ever to do this.

Instagram's great strength as a marketing tool isn't posting pictures of your product or putting clever quips over top of scenic landscapes. It's filling in the holes of your brand story that you might not have otherwise filled in. I post pictures of amazing food and even better beer, not because being a foodie or a brew enthusiast is related to what I do for a living but because it creates a more compelling story and point of view. It communicates my values, my passions, and my attention to details that matter to the people that matter to me.

During a trip to Orlando, Florida, I posted excitedly about a piece of crispy catfish I was eating at Cask & Larder, a nano brewery and "Southern Kitchen." Not only did this experience feel authentic to Florida, it felt like home (the Oregon Coast). I was surrounded by hipsters, amazing food, artisan cocktails, and killer beer. In sharing a moment like that, I leverage my Quiet Power over social media. It doesn't have to be on message; it doesn't even have to be on topic. It's filling in the details of my story in such a way that builds relationships and shares something deeply true about me with my audience.

Look at recent television successes like Sherlock, Walking Dead, or Downton Abbey. What makes these shows work? It's an irrepressible commitment to the world they've created and the unique perspective of the characters. Whether it's the way Benedict Cumberbatch plays Sherlock's sociopathic lovableness or the way the zombie threat stands in for all our personal fears or the exquisite attention to the details of propriety, dress, and service on display in an English manor house, these shows have chosen to fully invest in their unique points of view. When you get that all-too-familiar feeling that a show just isn't working, it's usually because the point of view of the world or the characters is off.

If you want your community and your customers to fully invest themselves in what you're creating, you need to be ready to fully invest in your unique point of view. You need to check all the details and add some when you find your story just isn't coming across. It's worth investing fully—your time, your money, and your energy—in experiences that make you more than a business, online and offline.

What product, marketing, sales, and management systems can you put in place to support and enhance your business's unique point of view?

The unique details of your story matter beyond surface level. That photo of crispy catfish and a delicious IPA is just a tiny morsel compared to all the ways I can use my passion for good food and beer in my business. Bear with me while I explain.

If I regularly tell stories about great eating and drinking experiences on social media and then you do business with me and come to an event I host, you expect that the event will in some way incorporate a great eating or drinking experience. I might host a dinner at one of the three local microbreweries in my tiny coastal town or I might have a local chef prepare a special meal for our get-together. At the same time, because these stories tell you more about my values (values that you likely share if you stick around), the experience doesn't even need to be food or drink related to be in alignment with what you'd expect. I might choose to create pleasurable, individualized customer service systems that make you feel just like the bartender has put your favorite brew on the bar as you settle on your barstool. I might also choose to create product systems that focus on personalization so that I can recommend the best place for you to start, just as a server might recommend the perfect wine to go with the dinner you've selected.

These aren't just examples; I have indeed made all of those choices in my business. My story and my business systems are integrated. This integration is a big part of what makes my business more compelling, and it is a major part of my own Quiet Power Strategy.

Or consider MailChimp. MailChimp is an email marketing service provider that specializes in beautiful design, high conversion, and just-plain-fun email marketing with a splash of mischief. Their mascot, Freddie the MailChimp, appears not only in their logo and visual branding, but sprinkled throughout the user interface. Before you confirm that you want to send an email, a sweaty chimp finger hovers over a big red button. Freddie tells jokes and suggests funny YouTube videos. He also hits physical mailboxes all over the world, showing up on knit caps and T-shirts and embodied in plush toys.

At every level of your interaction with MailChimp and its team, you get the sense that their marketing, product, sales, and management systems embody this sense of playfulness with a purpose. Their story and their strategic choices are completely integrated. Their support people are fun to interact with, their product people are clearly passionate about what they're developing, and their own email marketing is not only useful but beautiful and fun.

MailChimp's modus operandi is quintessentially Quiet Power Strategy. They're self-funded and chose to grow slowly and purposefully before they transitioned to a freemium model in 2009. They work their story and their desire to make email marketing fun into every layer and system of their business. Ben Chestnut, CEO and co-founder of MailChimp, says, "It's also kind of a cool idea to think of bajillions of 'serious' business newsletters being distributed with little monkeys in their footer."

Your business might not have fun as its chief value or craft beer among the unique passions you bring to your field. But whatever is most important to you and the customers you want to attract, make sure it is widely dispersed throughout every operation and every system of your business. That's the final key to developing a strategy that creates success for both you and the people who matter most to you.

The overall strategy for your business isn't the mix of tactics, formulas, or maps that you're going to use to succeed; it's the deep knowing–and the regular choices–that always points back to What You Want to Create and How You Want to Connect. Your strategic choices are rooted in your own Quiet Power. Those choices are, in fact, what makes you more powerful. It's not enough to have unique strengths, skills, and passion. We all have those. It is perceiving the multitude of options at your disposal, discerning your best opportunities, and focusing your actions on those opportunities that gives structure to the Quiet Power Strategy behind your business.

PART TWO:
SKILLS

Chapter 4

Perception

Tara Mohr is now a well-known expert in women's leadership and well-being and the author of Playing Big. But before that, she took a rather circuitous path. She started at Yale, got an MBA from Stanford, and did a stint in the non-profit sector. She's a certified life coach, too.

The thing about taking a circuitous path to power is that there are many opportunities for exploring and experimentation. Those opportunities lead to better understanding of What You Want to Create and How You Want to Connect. The path ends up being windy and seemingly indirect because you've allowed curiosity to guide you. Along the way, your Quiet Power begins to take root and your strategy starts coming ever so slightly into focus. On the path that Mohr took, she met many women. She listened to them, observed them, and became aware of patterns.

Mohr's observations allowed her to create a deep understanding of the women she wanted to serve. She identified the problems that were below the surface but acknowledged their more acute needs. The inflection point in the growth of her business and power was the development of the Playing Big brand. Starting as an online learning program and becoming a popular book, Playing Big is an answer to the perennial problem of women who "play small" because they're constantly trying to gain one more set of credentials, one more rung up the ladder. Women immediately flocked to the idea of Playing Big and a quietly powerful venture was born.

Mohr is perceptive. She uses all her senses—as well as her mind and her heart—to better understand the world around her. That perceptiveness leads to insights that crack open opportunities.

That's not how every business approaches the world or its customers. Instead, customer surveys, clinical market research, and the artificial environment of focus groups rule the day. But even in the depths of corporate America, an emphasis on keener perception is starting to take hold.

It's not uncommon for large organizations to employ the services of anthropologists today. It's not enough to focus-group what color or material customers want a product to be produced in. It's not enough to blast the latest marketing message across all channels. No, in the Social Era, nuance is king. Or queen.

Nuance, the subtle differences that help to distinguish one brand's story and ability to connect with customers from another brand's, can be the difference between a viral media campaign and a flopped product launch. Nuance comes from understanding exactly how customers use your product. It comes from understanding the meaning they assign to it. And those are things that can't be dictated by R&D departments or gargantuan marketing budgets.

But they can be researched, studied, and understood deeply using those budgets. Graeme Wood wrote about anthropological marketing research company ReD in The Atlantic: "ReD is one of just a handful of consultancies that treat everyday life—and everyday consumerism—as a subject worthy of the scrutiny normally reserved for academic social science. In many cases, the consultants in question have trained at the graduate level in anthropology but have forsaken academia—and some of its ethical strictures—for work that frees them to do field research more or less full-time, with huge budgets and agendas driven by corporate masters."

The good news is that the perceptiveness that Mohr leverages and the social science of companies like ReD aren't all that different. The internet of today gives us access to more social data than we've ever had at our disposal, allowing a perceptive business owner to understand not only what kinds of products her customers are looking for, but how they want to feel when they use them, who they aspire to be on a daily basis, and how they use those products as tools to accomplish what they really want.

Perceptive business owners develop business models and marketing systems that tap into those things. They leverage deep knowledge of both their customers and the world around them to craft products that feel familiar yet innovative, personalized yet community driven.

Perception or perceptiveness is the first core skill of self-leadership. You need to be extremely perceptive to be able to make the choices that add up to a powerful strategy. Without a doubt, it is the number one thing that separates people who leverage Quiet Power from those who don't. People who are perceptive, who work to understand the world around them and are constantly curious about others' worldviews, are one big step closer to getting ahead.

Unfortunately, many people have had their perceptiveness, like their self-leadership, beat out of them. Many of us are told—if not directly, then indirectly—to keep our heads down and mind our own business. We don't want to be nosy, we don't want to pry.

Instead of being perceptive, we make assumptions. We assume other people think the way we do, we assume people's actions are motivated by things that they're not. As we talked about earlier, making assumptions is a big roadblock for creative entrepreneurs, and it's a business killer. Assumptions harm our businesses internally just as they harm our relationships and our peace of mind.

When you react based on assumptions, you're almost always dealing with false information. Business owners charge low prices because they assume their customer base is overly price conscious. Marketers choose tired messages because they assume their targets have already bought into those messages. Entrepreneurs assume the conventional business model works because if everyone is doing it, it must be right.

But worst of all, assumptions trick you into thinking you know when you really don't. They turn off your ability to perceive what's actually happening. Your brain naturally seeks out information that confirms its biases, so you're left blind to what's really true.

So for many, perception is a skill that needs to be relearned and honed. How do you do that? Start listening. Stop worrying about how you're going to get the word out about your business, how you're going to connect with the right people, or how to get more people into your sales funnel.

Steve Blank, a serial entrepreneur, author, and leader within the Lean Startup movement, says it's important to "get out of the building" and observe your customers in their natural environments. Too often, entrepreneurs hole themselves away with their ideas, piling assumption on top of assumption on top of assumption.

Getting out of the building is about putting your perceptions—or assumptions—to the test. Instead of creating artificial environments where you invite customers or users in, you find real environments and you go out.

That means moving from your internal media platforms (email marketing, blogging, etc.) to external media platforms

(Facebook, Twitter, Pinterest, etc.). But it also means moving from digital to analog, photographic to tangible, online marketplace to physical marketplace. It can be as simple as taking someone who fits your ideal client profile out for drinks and asking truly curious questions about things other than the product you're bringing to market. It can also mean going to events full of potential consumers of your product and, instead of trying to answer everyone's questions, actually listening to what those questions are. Depending on your level of organization, you might catalog your learnings in spreadsheets and dossiers or simply tuck them away in your mental rolodex.

Learn to pay attention to all the turns of phrase, fears, hopes, and frustrations of the people your business serves. Don't hit them over the head with your insight before you've given them a chance to tell you everything that's on their minds. I know, that's hard for me, too.

I have found it's also extremely helpful to just show up as a human—as opposed to an entrepreneur or marketer—in these situations. When you are operating in your business, you tend to force the engagement using your analytical brain. Information comes in, analysis comes out. However, you have at your disposal a much more powerful device than your analytical brain, and that's your social brain.

As a social creature, your perceptiveness is already keen. Consider the last time you met someone new, had coffee with a friend, or supported a loved one through a rough situation. You likely didn't sit back and analyze what was happening. Instead, you largely relied on what we call intuition to guide your reactions, speech, and physical presence naturally. That intuition comes from tuning in to what you perceive in the situation—tone, body language, context, environment, etc.—and using it to guide your actions.

I'm fairly shy and introverted (I look for social situations where expectations are clear, and I have a difficult time molding myself to unusual situations) but I am still tolerably adept at handling social interaction without second-guessing myself at every turn. Conversation flows. Questions come and answers go. Much of the way I approach understanding my customers comes from what I pick up on during casual social interactions.

Once you've turned on your perceptiveness in social situations, you can start to apply it to the more analytical data you have on hand. You'll write better customer surveys, start reading between the lines of inquiries, and translating customer feedback into powerful statements of desire.

Honing your perceptiveness isn't just about your brain. Look up "perception" in the dictionary and you're likely to get a definition that marks perception as being about using all your senses to guide your understanding and insight. Perception is full-body awareness of what's really going on.

What we know on the surface can only guide us so far. If you want a better understanding of your customers' needs, feel into it. I wouldn't exactly suggest going with your gut, but paying attention to it sure can lead to deeper insights and more compelling action (more on that in Chapter 5).

When I asked my community who or what typified Quiet Power Strategy for them, Elizabeth Gilbert, the New York Times bestselling author of Eat, Pray, Love and The Signature of All Things, was mentioned early and often. Here is a great example of someone who grew into her Quiet Power Strategy. Before her breakaway book, she published a series of books and essays, both critically acclaimed and fairly popular. She built her reputation and platform from the ground up.

But Eat, Pray, Love was something else entirely. It tapped into an unrealized desire of American women to explore, find themselves, and flourish on their own terms. Whether that was planned or accidental didn't matter because Gilbert used her keen perception to keep the conversation flowing.

As I'm writing this, a friend remarked on Twitter that Elizabeth Gilbert is one of two reasons she's still on Facebook (the other being Anne Lamott). Gilbert's Facebook page is alive with activity and earnest sharing. She leverages perception to post exactly what her community needs to hear. Her brand has flourished, not just because she is a talented writer, but because she's chosen to show up and use her perception to answer her audience's burning questions.

Perception drives compelling conversation. It motivates innovative solutions. It answers the call because it hears the call. Even when it's whispered.

Without engaging perceptiveness, Quiet Power Strategy falls flat. If seeing, hearing, and understanding below the surface isn't one of your strong suits, you can use an exercise from the Lean Startup methodology to jumpstart your insights.

It's called the Five Whys and it's defined in Eric Ries's book, The Lean Startup: "The core idea of Five Whys is to tie investments directly to the prevention of the most problematic symptoms. The system takes its name from the investigative method of asking the question 'Why?' five times to understand what has happened (the root cause)." The role of perceptiveness is not just identifying the root causes of problems, but getting to the root of any frustration, fear, or desire.

Getting to the root of what you're perceiving opens your mind to deeper understanding. That leads to more creative insights. Whatever your initial observation, ask yourself "Why?" over and over again to get to the root of what you're perceiving.

Perception is the first core skill of Quiet Power Strategy because without it, there is no way to discern your next steps or focus your actions.

Chapter 5

Discernment

My partner, Sean, works as a server at a brewery. He's a master who sees service as a craft, not just a job. When he approaches a new table, he uses his power of perception to take in an immense amount of data. Are they excited about being at a favorite brewery? Just trying to feed the kids before they head to the beach? Are they industry people? Are they in a hurry or wanting to linger?

When you've been doing this work for as long as Sean has, you know what to look for. The signs—the whispers, the smiles, the questions, the enthusiasm or lack thereof—are obvious. For Sean, it's not just about perceiving what the situation is but using it for his benefit. Luckily, he's a server that understands his benefit is generally received by creating the best experience for his customers.

He also understands that each customer's "best experience" is different. The family who's just trying to get hot dogs into the kids before they head to the beach wants fast service and no nonsense. The couple who is on a beer tour of the North Coast doesn't want to be rushed and is very happy to listen to a lengthy description of everything on tap. The blogger who's out from Portland wants the insider information and thinks he deserves to be treated like a rock star.

Sean perceives the situation and discerns the best course of action to create the experience the customers want. Ideally, this leads to a much bigger tip at the end of the meal.

Discernment isn't just decision-making. Discernment is using what you perceive in the environment around you to choose action or direction that's grounded in who you are, what you want, and the experience you're creating for customers. How do you ensure you get the best results when choosing between two equally correct paths? Discernment.

There are many ways to hone your skill of discernment. Danielle LaPorte's Desire Map system is one of them. She says, "A powerful choice is one that includes your mind, your body, your spirit, and your heart." If that's your compass for creating strategy, it's a very fine compass indeed.

According to *The Desire Map*, the key to personal power and success is getting clear on how you want to feel. What feelings are you trying to cultivate in your life? When you're faced with choices, you lean into the course of action that will help you cultivate those feelings.

Another system for discernment is somatic psychology. I first learned about this method from Dr. Susan Bernstein, creator of The Sensational Shift. She helps her clients and workshop participants by guiding them to feel into decisions. Instead of thinking things through with only their heads, she helps them to "bring the elevator down" and draw attention to the sensations they feel throughout their bodies. Our bodies might be the ultimate barometers of what is true for us, what's true of our desires, and how we'll best serve the people who buy from us.

I asked Dr. Bernstein about the best way to get started with discernment using your body. She said, "Start to notice your own signature way of sensing a decision." Just like there's no "right" way to go about building your business, there is no "right" way to feel into a decision. You need to focus on what your way is going to be. She continued, "When you're making choices, pay attention to your breathing—is it shallow or deep? Where do you tense up? How does your chest feel? Your stomach? Are you hot or cold? Then, put a hand on the area of your body where the sensations are most prominent (or imagine that body region, if it's hard or awkward to touch). Ask your body, 'What wisdom do you have for me about this decision?'" She suggested listening for a voice that doesn't feel like your regular voice but instead is the unique voice of your embodied consciousness. With practice, you can get better and better at tuning into that voice.

I also asked Dr. Bernstein how to tell whether those butterflies in my stomach mean something good or something bad when I'm trying to discern my next step. Those common physical signals can come from positively venturing out of your comfort zone, but they can also come from genuine fear or misgivings. Bernstein suggests getting really specific with that butterfly feeling: "Are you feeling gripping? Stabbing? Where is the sensation? How, if at all, does it move? The more you can describe the sensation, the more you'll start to recognize that you've got energy in you, and that as you pay neutral attention to it, that energy shifts and communicates with you." Our bodies have a lot to tell us and can help us leverage discernment when our minds are feeling confused.

Still others discern through intuition. I've worked with many clients who specialize in intuition and have come to understand that intuition is a finely honed skill of perception. Tracey Selingo, creator of Woo School, believes we all have the power to tap into intuition as a means of discerning the best path. She says, "Intuition is defined as the ability to understand something immediately, without proof or reasoning to believe said something is so. Intuition is a six-sense experience. You have six senses: sight, hearing, taste, smell, touch, and subtle energy."

It stands to reason that if we're actively honing our sensory perception and concurrently tapping into a more internal truth about ourselves, we're better prepared to make use of this sixth sense to guide our courses of action. Tracey brings it home, "Your intuitive powers are directly related to your source of empowerment."

If discernment is so easy to access, why do we have such a difficult time using it to guide our action on a daily basis? It's less that we're bad decision-makers and more that we're out of touch with the things that are truly the useful guides. Whether you choose Desire Mapping, sensational psychology, intuition, or your own brand of knowing the right way, each requires that you really know what you want and where you're headed.

Unfortunately, the stress of running a business often puts you in a reactive mode rather than a proactive mode. You can't leverage discernment when you're reacting to outside circumstances. When you're dealing with a customer complaint, a less-than-exciting P&L report, or a flopped sales conversation, it's nearly impossible to stay grounded in who you are, what you want, and what kind of experience you want to create for your customers.

That's why every business owner needs to make time for understanding these things. Once you know What You Want to Create and How You Want to Connect, you need to make sure it's always top of mind and guiding your process of discernment. That could be as simple as a note on your computer or a poster on your office wall. Once you're clear on your strategic plan, it's time to communicate it to the team. What do they need to know about what's true for you and the business, the goals you have as a team, and the experience you're mutually creating for your customers?

When the whole team is clear on this, they're much more empowered to discern their own course of action and require much less management from you. Nilofer Merchant—the same thinker who brought us Onlyness—writes, "When people know the purpose of an organization, they don't need to check in or get permission to take the next step; they just create value." Even more so when they understand the innate strategy and story a business is working to co-create with its customers.

Now, when I say that knowing what's true about you, what you want, and the experience you want to create for your customer is the key to discernment, this is not a woo-woo sort of knowing. This isn't just a "I know who I am deep down in my bones" sort of feeling. I would never discount the importance of such things, but, without specificity, that kind of knowing doesn't guide action or decision-making.

What's true about you? Grape or strawberry jelly? Star Trek or Star Wars? Stripes or polka dots? Natalie or Scarlett? Ben or Matt? Vanilla or chocolate?

What's true of what you want? Legacy or exit strategy? Five high-paying clients or 10,000 people buying your book?

What's true of the experience you're creating for customers? How do you want them to feel after working with you or consuming your product? What details are important to you?

Once you are clear on these things, you can communicate the foundation of your strategy to your team with that clarity.

I've always been incredibly impressed with the discernment that Sarah J. Bray, web strategist, founder of A Small Nation, and resident nation-builder at &yet, has displayed with her business and creative endeavors. She has chosen to pivot on projects, businesses, and her career with the utmost elegance at times when others would have pushed through. When she has explained her actions, I'm always blown away by her understanding of precisely what she wants, what she wants to create, and who she wants to create for. Her ability to leverage discernment to get closer and closer to the life and work she truly wants to realize is second to none.

Over the years that I've been following and friends with Sarah, I've seen her pivot a web design studio, launch multiple programs, found a digital "nation-building" agency, and move into full-time employment with an app design company. While some might see this as reflecting a lack of focus or intention, for Sarah, it's just the opposite. It's a deliberate process of discernment and careful self-inquiry that leads to every decision, every change of direction. Her personal Quiet Power Strategy is clear and yet always open to new information and more powerful choices.

On my own blog, I once wrote about her that she represented the pinnacle of both digital honesty and unflinching ambition. Sarah told me that the key to her ever-evolving body of work is to "treat it like an experiment," which is not to say that she throws spaghetti at a wall to see what sticks. No, she uses a true process of experimentation to create, analyze, and iterate on her work. In a way, discernment is key to this type of experimentation. It's not enough to just "give it a try," you have to carefully determine your variables, understand your metrics for success, and take time to assign value to the information you get from the experiment.

Did it bring you closer to where you're headed? Did it help you achieve something closer to what you ultimately want to create? Did it provide the experience you want for your customers? By addressing these questions, you incorporate a sort of creative scientific method into your work that guides your focus based on what you've learned.

Now, speaking of focus, let's move on to the third skill of Quiet Power Strategy.

Chapter 6

Focus

I've worked with and observed hundreds of entrepreneurs over the last 5 years. One of the biggest factors that predicts future success is the ability to focus. Focus is not just the ability to block out distractions but to create the right conditions for uncompromising progress towards one's goal. That probably sounds exhausting. Yet one of the key conditions for that kind of productivity is to discover what energizes and motivates you, then leverage it to your advantage.

There are many enemies to this kind of focus today. Beyond the usual suspects of technological distractions and ever-shortening attention spans, there's a silent killer: too many goals. Manifold goal setting has become a panacea for a lack of clarity and purpose. The more goals you have the more productive you can be, right? Wrong.

Hyper goal setting is similar to the curse of busyness; they are both highly desirable yet completely useless states of modern living. If you find yourself answering, "I'm busy" every time someone asks how you're doing, you know this well. Modern life asks us to wear busyness like a badge of honor. Yet the busier we become, the less we're actually creating.

Tim Kreider, writing in the New York Times, claims that while we'd expect to hear complaints of busyness from ER doctors or minimum wage workers pulling back-to-back shifts to make ends meet, "It's almost always people whose lamented busyness is purely self-imposed: work and obligations they've taken on voluntarily, classes and activities they've 'encouraged' their kids to participate in. They're busy because of their own ambition or drive or anxiety, because they're addicted to busyness and dread what they might have to face in its absence." What do we face in the absence of busyness? The imperative to create, innovate, or transform. Busyness as usual is far less frightening.

We keep busy and set more and more goals because we're bored. "To be bored isn't to be indifferent. It is to be fatigued. Because one is exhausted," writes Umair Haque, an economist and thought leader on the next era of capitalism. We're exhausted by the relentless pace of keeping up with the market, others' expectations, and evolving "norms" that leave everyone feeling less than normal. We constantly layer more and more "work" onto our calendars, our kids' schedules, and our doggy's day books to find meaning in a world where there seems to be none. Keeping busy feels more comfortable than trusting a strategy or opening yourself to the space that fosters creative possibilities.

We search and search for fulfillment, purpose, and meaning. But meaning—usefulness, even—isn't found. It's created.

While we quest endlessly, we put up with a reality that falls short of what's possible. Haque continues, "[We want to be] liked, not loved ... clever, not wise; snarky, not happy; advantaged, not prosperous." It looks good on paper—your résumé, your Facebook profile, your brochure—but it doesn't fulfill you.

In your business, hyper goal setting and chronic busyness results in innovation taking a backseat to getting stuff done and meaningful marketing losing out to the hot new thing. Of course, it's not that getting stuff done and learning new methods are bad. That's what's so dangerous about this problem. Yet if you haven't stopped and focused on what you're really trying to create and how you'd really like to connect with your customers, you will lose out on the opportunity to do something truly beautiful, wise, or prosperous.

Focus is what allows us to inhabit the quiet spaces where power resides.

To truly focus, you need to edit. Edit your vision for happiness, edit the number of features your new widget comes with, edit the way you communicate with your team, edit the number of appointments on your calendar. Most importantly, edit the number of goals you set. Edit the number of things you're trying to accomplish at any one time.

Once you find yourself in the quiet space that an edited life and business affords you, you can tap into the power that allows you to act on the imperative to create, innovate, and transform. You can build something that truly matters to the people who matter most to you.

Of course, focus isn't about just clearing space; it's about taking action. Another problem with hyper goal setting is complete paralysis when it comes to deciding what to do next. I believe that lacking a clear focus is a much bigger problem than a genuine lack of ability to prioritize. Think about your team or a group that you've managed in the past. Consider a time when you wish your subordinates had been better able to prioritize their actions. Maybe they took action on one assignment when you would have wanted them to prioritize another. Or maybe they prioritized a company policy in their customer communications when you would have preferred they prioritize the customer's satisfaction.

Why did that happen? Is it because they were truly lacking in the ability to prioritize? Or was it because you had not provided focused leadership on what was ultimately important to you and the business? Likely it was the latter. If this is an endemic problem among managers and teams, what happens when you have to manage yourself? What happens when you're in charge of yourself, when you are the person you need to lead?

Often clients come to me with the complaint that they don't know what to prioritize in their businesses. Their self-leadership stagnated sometime after getting their venture off the ground. They've got big plans and they're trying to tackle them all at once. They don't know what action to take next because most things they've tried to this point have left them wanting for more progress. It's not that the action they took was bad; it's that the goal—the very point of that action—was ill-defined because it was part of a whole cadre of equally important mile markers that don't have a clear connection to their mission as business owners and entrepreneurs. Penelope Trunk, blogger and founder of Brazen Careerist, writes, "I talk to so many people who say they don't know what they should do next. But actually they just don't have the guts to close off options. The key to committing to a goal is to understand that you will not be trapped, because taking options away from yourself actually opens up more possibilities."

When Stacey Howe-Lott, the SAT strategist you met in Chapter 2, started working with me, she knew she wanted to scale her business to help more kids get remarkable scores. For as hard as she brainstormed, she just couldn't find a way around working with kids in a one-on-one approach. She believed the personalized attention she was able to give her students was what allowed them to achieve such extraordinary results (she helps kids score hundreds of points higher in less than 10 hours of tutoring). Through a process of perception and discernment, we figured out that it wasn't her personalized attention but her strategic, analysis-based approach to test-taking that allowed her students to see such impressive results.

While this might not seem like a big deal on the surface, the implications for Stacey were huge. Instead of focusing on personalizing her approach for clients based on her test-taking strategy, she could focus on teaching the strategy and sharing her analytical toolkit so that students could personalize the approach for themselves. With that clarity of focus, Stacey started on a whirlwind series of actions that has allowed her to see massive growth, and to build tools and resources that have the capacity to revolutionize the test prep industry. What's more, while Stacey is working incredibly hard, she remains energized and motivated. She doesn't feel like she's just busy; she feels like she's making real progress toward her goal.

Focus is elusive. When it feels like your business is pulling you in a hundred directions at once, when it seems like your team can't prioritize what's most important, when not even you know what action is going to create lasting results, focus seems like a luxury. But it doesn't have to be that way. Business owners who leverage Quiet Power Strategy block out the Noise of the rest of the world and zero in on a guiding goal. They prioritize based on the one thing that inspires them. They have a singular focus on what they're creating. They lead themselves.

Above all else, what do you want to build, achieve, or create over the next year? What is that one objective that will keep you motivated and inspired even when you're doing tasks that don't light you up? What is important to you, not the market or the community?

When it comes to focus, it's not a time for generously leaving yourself open to possibilities; it's time for checking in with what drives you and using that as your singular focus. I call this focus your Chief Initiative. It's the driving force behind all other actions in your business. If a task, tactic, or activity isn't getting you one small step closer to achieving your Chief Initiative, it's got to go.

Your Chief Initiative is what allows you to make sure your tactical planning lines up with something that truly motivates you and keeps you on target instead of aimed at meaningless metrics or milestones. To start creating your tactical plan, first figure out what conditions define your Chief Initiative. These conditions are the embodiment and environment of the success of your Chief Initiative. Who is surrounding you in your success? What does it feel like? How are your day-to-day actions different? How is your environment? Often, achieving a big, hairy goal changes a lot of things. Knowing what those changes are allows you to start implementing many of them now. Those forward-looking changes can be a source of ease and confidence, as well as a North Star as you work toward your Chief Initiative.

Then, consider what smaller goals you need to accomplish to make your Chief Initiative a reality. Want to write a book and get a book deal? "Land an agent" should be one of your goals. Want to sell out your next product launch? "Build my email list by 50%." Want to give a TED talk? "Speak to 20 local organizations." Every big goal has baby steps, smaller milestones that need to be achieved. Make a list of the things that, even if not required, would make your Chief Initiative that much closer or more realistic. You should be able to simplify these goals into a list of straightforward tasks. If you can't, drill down further to find more concrete milestones.

Next, consider the systems you need to put in place to make the regular tasks—like social media marketing or client management—behind your Chief Initiative easier and less energy intensive. Your systems might vary widely depending on your industry and the Initiative you're working toward. One system that has been extremely important in my business is my system for lead generation, which last year led to surpassing my Chief Initiative of 100% revenue growth. Instead of trying a bunch of things all at once, I've carefully honed in over the years on which tactics deliver the best results for my business and also allow me the greatest fun. Instead of putting lots of energy into blanket lead generation, I can focus that energy into the 2 or 3 tactics that work best and plan that energy out through the course of the year.

Finally, think about the people you need to enlist in the cause. In order to achieve your Chief Initiative, you might need to build your team or replace a weak link. Many business owners underestimate how important their teams are when it comes to achieving next-level goals. The longer you're in business and the more you strive for success, the more you need to rely on others, even as you ground the business further in your own Quiet Power.

With the help of your Chief Initiative strategy, you can drill down through your overarching motivation, the conditions you need to change to embody that goal, the concrete goals you need to achieve to make it all happen, the systems you can put in place to make it all more easeful, and the people you need to surround yourself with to connect with the outcomes. You've turned an immense amount of work into a focused plan you can lead yourself—as well as your team and customer base—through.

Danielle LaPorte, the creator of the Desire Map system that I mentioned in the previous chapter, leverages tremendous focus as both an individual and a brand. With two successful books, *The Fire Starter Sessions* and *The Desire Map*, LaPorte has any number of avenues to explore. In early 2014, she was promising a new venture: Danielle magazine. She hired an editor, chose the paper, had photographs taken and articles written. She spent over $100,000 in development. Then she put it in the can. Why? "Devotion to my currently awesome reality wins. It came down to focus. And lifestyle. And grace," she wrote on her blog.

She could have plugged along. She could have continued to juggle her "currently awesome reality" with her new dreams of self-expression. She could have had a beautiful creative product with Danielle magazine, but instead she chose to double down on her existing creative projects and has created a masterful suite of products related to *The Desire Map*—including licensing opportunities, card decks, audio programs, candles, and malas—through her focus. And just because she chose to shelve the magazine now doesn't mean that path isn't available to her in the future. Focus isn't so much about saying "no" as it is saying "not now."

Focus requires difficult choices, choices that eliminate some of your options. For a creative person, this can be scary. I like keeping my options open as much as the next person, but I know that not taking straight-and-narrow strategic direction in my business makes traction much more difficult and lasting success near impossible.

Focus is knowing where you're heading and giving yourself the permission to take the straightest path there. It's leading yourself with the determination, tenacity, and ambition you and your ideas deserve. Finally, focus is a regular process of gut-checking and self-inquiry that allows you to know when you've been led astray by those same positive traits.

Focus is what turns perception and discernment into action. It's what keeps you from constantly being in analysis mode. It turns Quiet Power Understanding into Quiet Power Strategy.

Chapter 7

How to Create Your Quiet Power Strategic Plan

If you've made it this far in the book and still feel a bit steamrolled by all the options you have for your business, I can assure you that you're not alone. At this point, you should have considered the 5 strategic questions I posed. You've probably also taken stock of your natural abilities of perception, discernment, and focus. No matter where you're starting from, the important thing is that you're starting. You can evolve from there. As Roger Martin writes in Playing to Win, "Strategy is an iterative process in which all of the moving parts influence one another and must be taken into account together."

When I work with a client to coach them through strategic planning, they see immediate results. Then, almost without fail, they come back 3, 6, or 12 months later with a new revelation that transforms their business—they've perceived something going on in the market or they've discerned that a next step we thought was obvious wasn't the right one. So they adjust their strategy, reevaluate how that affects the other parts of their business, and then reap the benefits. Those immediate results from our initial work may be good, but what comes later ends up being even better.

Creating your Quiet Power Strategy isn't a one-time thing. It's not even an annual process. By continually honing your skills of perception, discernment, and focus, your Quiet Power Strategy will evolve over time. You'll discover new things about the world around you and what you want, and you'll make adjustments. Don't try to get it "right" the first time; just get something down on paper that feels good and makes sense with the information you have now.

This is a good time to remind you that strategy and tactics are two very different things. Strategy is the foundation—the why—and tactics are what you build on top of that foundation—the what and how. Take one look around the entrepreneurial corners of the internet and you'll find thousands of ideas about great tactics for business growth. Up until now, you've probably been cherry picking the tactics that seemed most useful or successful, and you've found that sometimes they work, sometimes they don't. When you focus on strategy first, you can more effectively select or create the tactics that will realize that strategy and your vision. As a result, your success rate will go up quite a bit.

Before you start constructing your Quiet Power Strategy, do a quick warm-up by considering the following questions and scenarios. This will prime your brain for discovering key insights about the opportunities in your business.

First, reflect on a time when you've been especially effective in persuading someone to agree with you. Think you're not a great salesperson? Hate the idea of being "salesy"? Salesy is what happens when you try to use persuasion techniques that aren't natural to you. You have a natural way of getting buy in from others and you've used it throughout your life. Unfortunately, you probably think you have to do something different when it comes to your business. Not so. You can use your natural method of persuasion in your business, too.

When I was growing up, my mother had a clothing alterations business. She would often encounter customers who assumed they knew how their pants should be hemmed or how much a dress should be taken in. That's understandable. But as she so often does, my mom knew better. In order to persuade a customer, she would demonstrate her position by pinning the garment to where she felt it looked best. Demonstration has always been my mom's best persuasion method. If she can show you her perspective, she's very likely to get you on board.

Next, consider what personal principle or value heavily influences the way you approach your work or life. Think about how that personal principle makes your approach different than others. The unique value sets you bring to life and work help to differentiate you from others and make what you do a better fit for the right people.

Shawn Fink, creator of the Abundant Mama Project, has a personal value of playfulness. Mixing that with her principles for living slow and incorporating deep reflection into daily life gives her a unique perspective. Her approach to parenting and mamahood stands out in a sea of mommy blogs and parenting experts and has earned her a large, loyal following.

Then think about what conditions make it easy for you to meet new people. For some of us, meeting people comes easily. But for many, it can be a bit nerve-wracking. When you know how meeting new people works for you, you can work to incorporate those conditions into your business so that your networking, lead generation, and community-building comes more naturally and winds up being much more effective.

For me, meeting people becomes easier when I am given a little more time to respond to conversation and have more information about the person I'm meeting. That means social media has been a godsend, as well as a chief networking and lead generation tool in my business. I can pace responses and do a little research if necessary in the course of building a new relationship. On the other hand, my friend and collaborator Brigitte Lyons, founder of B, a PR agency, prefers a faster pace for meeting new people. She can work a room like nobody's business, but where she really excels is in meeting one or two people at a time and engaging them in personal conversation. She does fine on social media but gets amazing results at conferences or meetups.

Next, consider how you like others to respond to you or your ideas when they're working with you. Some people prefer exuberant validation and enthusiasm. Others prefer thoughtful critique and great questions. Some are looking for immediate action. Others are quite happy with deep introspection. Knowing how you want people to respond allows you to create systems in your business that encourage those responses and appeal to the right people for your business.

One way I love people to respond to my own work is with questions. I like validation, I love enthusiasm, but what really makes me happy is people wanting to know more. So I incorporate the opportunity for my community and customers to respond with questions in all of my marketing and programs. Plus, I know that I shine when others put me on the spot. This system makes the work I do stand out from the rest of the field.

Finally, reflect on who inspires you to create or serve the way you and your business do. The people who inspire us shed light on the systems and tactics we can use to be more effective. When you look to draw inspiration from others, don't necessarily look to industry leaders; look to the people who inspire you in all areas of life and work. They're likely the people whose systems and method of operating are most closely aligned with your own. Don't just expect others to get you and your unique brand of crazy. Take the time to identify it and name it for them.

One of my clients, Dr. Jessica Michaelson, a parenting expert who works with parents to help them express themselves and feel more confident, looks to comedian Louis CK for inspiration. She finds his mix of honest self-deprecation with a generous side of good-natured humor refreshing and encouraging. Jason Zinoman, reviewing a show by CK in the New York Times, recently wrote, "He has found countless laughs over agony and loathing, from his own immoral thoughts to his unstoppable gluttony." It's this kind of levity that Dr. Jessica brings to her clients during the trials of parenthood. Even when they're feeling at the end of their proverbial rope, she creates a space for them to see light amidst the dark.

As I've mentioned, I look to Tina Fey. Her brand of smart but sometimes crude, timely but sometimes esoteric comedy inspires the way I approach the subjects I love. Fey says, "You can tell how smart people are by what they laugh at." I want my work to always feel approachable and balanced. I want it to be both edgy and practical. I want others to feel both smart and accepted when they engage my work, my clients, and my community.

It's essential to consider the scenarios I just discussed before trying to construct your plan because your Quiet Power Strategy must be based on what's true for you—what makes you unique and effective, what you choose instead of what you affect. You don't want to be influenced by what you perceive as the "shoulds" of your market or industry. This is your opportunity to redefine the way business is done in your market, not for the sake of innovation but for the sake of your own effectiveness. Don't allow the status quo to impact your plan; that will only stifle your ability to see new paths forward. You're not at the mercy of the market. You're in control.

There is one final step to complete before creating your Quiet Power Strategy plan. That step is to define what success looks like to you both in terms of your own business and in terms of the customers you serve. You've already considered your strategic vision and chosen a Chief Initiative.

Revisit your idea of success one more time. One common roadblock to true success for many entrepreneurs is the allure of others' success. You can't define what you want by what others have achieved. Sure, a healthy knowledge of what's possible can help you expand your success horizons, but to construct your vision of success you don't want to rely on what you feel like you "should" want.

Your idea of success doesn't need to be set in stone, but it does need to be something that provides direction to your daily activities and recharges your personal motivation when you're feeling down.

Part and parcel with your own vision of success is the vision of success you have for your customers. You began considering this in Chapter 3 and a healthy business considers this often. How do you want their lives to be different because of working with your business? What effects do you want to see in their world because of your product or service? Making sure your vision for your customers is incorporated into your strategic plan means that you'll be working toward that transformation on a daily basis.

Your strategic plan is the foundational set of choices that will influence every other choice you make in your business. As you construct your strategic plan, you'll decide What You Want to Create and How You Want to Connect impacts Who You Create For and How They Respond. Each choice influences the next. There is no 1, 2, 3, 4 step plan. While you set about making individual choices, pull back and make sure those choices help to tell an overall story about your strategic success. By understanding the choices you make—and by making choices proactively instead of reactively—you have the capacity to lead your business where you want it to go instead of just responding to outside pressure.

What You Want to Create

Your strategic plan begins by determining What You Want to Create. Just like every other piece of this puzzle, it's not What You Think You Should Create or What Seems to Be Making Other Businesses Successful. This is about how you choose to bring value to the market. It's about solving a problem or creating something desirable in that way only you can.

Of course, it's not just What You Want to Create but about where you see need, or where you see your itch to create lining up with what people have use for. You don't get carte blanche to create whatever you want and call it a strategy. You do get to use the needs and desires of others to inspire and inform what you want to create and bring to market.

One way to do this is to examine what others are saying, doing, thinking, and feeling. I have all of my clients complete a Perspective Map to record what they perceive in the market. It looks like this:

SAY	DO
THINK	FEEL

To complete this exercise, observe what your customers do or say (outside of their relationship with you or your business) in an effort to address their need, frustration, or desire. For instance, if you're looking to serve customers who want to up their fitness level, you might record that they:

- Say their feet hurt at the end of a run
- Say they wish they could wear their running shoes as casual shoes
- Do keep running clothes stashed in their car
- Do go running whenever the mood strikes
- Think they'd like to incorporate more workouts into their life if only it wasn't so inconvenient
- Feel vibrant when they finish a workout
- Feel satisfied when they end their day having really used their bodies

Through these observations, you might discover that what your customers really need is for you to create a cute pair of running shoes that also provides great support. They could wear them on a regular basis and easily transition to workouts so they can experience more vibrancy and satisfaction on a daily basis. Or if you were more into designing accessories than sneakers, you might create a new bag that allowed customers to easily keep their workout gear handy as well as easily spruce up when the workout was over. There are many possibilities and each is a viable option to explore.

The key is to define What You Want to Create based on Where You See Need. Let's face it: it's easier to get creative when we have context and constraints. It's much more difficult to be creative in an open-ended environment. Embrace the constraints but give yourself full rein over what you choose to create within those constraints.

Next, consider what conversation your business is a part of. As we talked about before, the book *The Cluetrain Manifesto* lists "Markets are conversations" as its first thesis on doing business in the age of the internet. Consumers today have a base expectation of being not just sold at (read:

told what to buy) but engaged by the brands that market to them. When you're determining What You Want to Create it's important to consider how what you create will shape or impact the conversation your business participates in.

If you're a yoga instructor, your business participates in conversations about yoga, fitness, wellness, and personal development. If you're a potter, your business participates in conversations about home decor, slow living, and entertaining. If you're a management consultant, your business participates in conversations about management, business, and entrepreneurship.

While your business might participate in multiple conversations, the conversation you choose to focus on for marketing, outreach, and product/offer development helps you direct your efforts in a consistent manner. For instance, the marketing and offer development for a yoga business focused on a fitness conversation is going to look very different than a yoga business focused on a personal development conversation. A pottery business focused on a home decor conversation is going to approach marketing very differently than a pottery business focused on a slow living conversation.

Consider the conversation or conversations you identified in Chapter 3. You may now see opportunities you didn't see before. Each path is equally valid, so choose the conversation you want to participate in. Choose a dialogue that's going to keep you motivated and engaged when it comes to marketing.

Once you know the conversation you want to participate in, you need to incorporate the vision you've developed into your business's voice in the conversation. By being in business, you have a position of leadership in the market. Not only do you need to exercise your self-leadership, you need to exercise market leadership. Your vision for where you want to take your customers and the conversation you're having allows you to lead with more power. Your vision need not be grandiose. Your vision might be about more ease, less frustration, or simply a better way to do something.

Consider how the vision you have helps to differentiate your business from the rest of the market. Your vision for ease might separate your business in a conversation focused overwhelmingly on price. Your vision for innovation could distinguish your business in a conversation focused on tradition. Look for each way your business stands out from the rest of the conversation and leverage those differences to your advantage when it comes to positioning, promotion, and product development.

In considering each part of What You Want to Create, you'll use your skills of perception, discernment, and focus. First, you perceive both what exists and what is true for you. Then, you discern how you'll approach the overlap between existing needs and your desire to create. Finally, you'll choose areas of focus that lead your business to differentiate and capture loyalty among potential customers.

How You Want to Connect

One of the greatest misconceptions about promotional tactics is that there is a certain set of maneuvers that work. Maybe you believe there is a secret plan that everyone who is successful is following and that if only you could get on the inside and follow that plan in your own business, you too would find that kind of success. Not so. If there is any kind of secret, it's that different businesses use different tactics to connect with their customers in a way that supports and reinforces their unique makeup, positioning, and vision, and that is precisely why those tactics work for them.

Take two entrepreneurs supporting small and micro business today: Marie Forleo and Laura Roeder. Both women are using social media to their advantage. Both women support entrepreneurs and business owners. Both women leverage online learning to generate revenue. However, they approach promotion very differently. Forleo uses a weekly high-production-value web TV show to build an audience and connect with potential customers. Altogether, her videos have upwards of 11 million views. Her fans eagerly await each new episode, and when she announces enrollment for her signature B-School program, they respond in droves.

Roeder, on the other hand, predominantly connects with customers through the LKR Social Media blog and her email newsletter. The blog is filled with both her team's and outside voices while the newsletter is her voice and perspective. Occasionally Roeder appears on video for a promotional or educational opportunity, but the majority of her platform growth is fueled through the blog and email newsletter.

Each woman is running a multimillion-dollar business. Each is well-respected in her field. But because of the unique makeup of their businesses, the personal perspective they bring to platform growth, and distinct strengths each has in regards to how they connect with people, they choose different means of connecting with prospects. They've discovered how they are individually most effective and aren't interested in tactics that don't play to their strengths.

Further, the way they've chosen to connect influences the way their businesses develop offers. LKR Social Media offers a membership community run by a team of experts and influencers. They also recently developed an automation and planning app for social media. In contrast, Marie Forleo International focuses on video-based learning and luxury events. The way each business chooses to connect in marketing determines how it connects with customers through its offers and vice versa. Marketing and product development today must be integrated and based on the unique strengths of how a business naturally connects with its potential customer base.

If you feel uncomfortable promoting your products or delivering your services, there is a good chance you've followed someone else's lead on connecting with your customers instead of your own. It's your choice How You Want to Connect with others, and it's one of the most important choices you'll make in your business because it helps determine so much of your overall business strategy.

The other big misconception about marketing is that you can rely on What You Want to Create to inspire connection with potential customers. Gabriel Weinberg and Justin Mares, authors of the book *Traction: A Startup Guide to Getting Customers*, write, "Many entrepreneurs think that if you build a killer product, your customers will beat a path to your door. We call this line of thinking The Product Trap: the fallacy that the best use of your time is always improving your product. In other words, 'if you build it, they will come' is wrong." Connection needs to be part of your strategy and you need a plan for it.

There are more ways to connect with potential customers today than ever before, and that can feel overwhelming. Start by considering how you and your business naturally connect with new customers. Maybe in-person sales has worked best for you. Maybe referrals have been effective. Maybe your team has a knack for creating viral videos. Think about what means of connecting have received the most traction and produced the most results without a lot of hassle or stress.

Then, consider what personal values or guiding principles help you define your relationships, both personally and professionally. What shared values make a friendship or coworking relationship go from good to great for you? What unspoken rules naturally guide the way you relate to others? Reflect on how these personal values are represented in your business and how you can use them to create more effective marketing tactics.

One of my clients, Jacquette Timmons, is a financial behaviorist and the author of Financial Intimacy. Timmons believes that financial success isn't just about managing what's happening in your wallet and your bank account. She has personal values of depth and wisdom and she brings that into the way she connects with prospective clients. During her monthly Financial Intimacy Hour calls, she dives into the subjects that influence the way we earn, spend, and invest money in a way that makes clear her imperative to communicate the multiple facets of wealth. Her listeners don't just receive more money advice; they receive wisdom that influences their whole money story. Timmons uniquely positions herself and her business in a very saturated market by allowing her personal values to influence the way she connects with her customer base.

Similarly, you can look to your unique point of view to guide the way you choose to connect with prospects. What do you see that other providers in your market don't see? What does your solution do differently than other solutions? How does your solution work differently than other solutions? As I mentioned in Chapter 3, MailChimp uses their unique point of view (that email marketing should be fun) to connect with their customers. From clever graphics hidden throughout the interface like Easter Eggs, to giveaways of physical products, they've spread goodwill about their product and brand in ways that simply wouldn't work for other email marketing providers.

In the example I used at the beginning of this section, Marie Forleo uses video because it allows her to connect with her audience on multiple levels. It's not just about the business and life advice but about her personal style, her wacky sense of humor, and her connections with other influencers. Those things make up a truly unique point of view in her field, and video is the perfect medium for creating that connection.

When you consider how you'll approach How You Want to Connect, think about the media that's most appropriate for your values and point of view as well as the way you'll represent your unique makeup as a business. Reflect on the kind of relationship you want to cultivate with prospects and customers as they maneuver through your business. Finally, think about what tactics would reinforce the story you want others to tell about your business, its values, and the way it solves problems.

Who You Want to Create For

Quiet Power Strategy is an integrated set of choices you make about how you lead yourself and your business. While it might seem like What You Want to Create and How You Want to Connect can stand on their own as the core focus of your strategy, they won't be as effective or successful if you don't integrate Who You Want to Create For into the choices you make. After all, you can buy a birthday gift for 3 different people, but you'd choose to buy 3 different gifts and present them in 3 different ways. If you don't choose who your business is creating for at the same time you make choices about what you're creating and how you're going to connect with people to get it in their hands, your efforts are likely to fall flat.

The biggest mistake I see people make when it comes to who they want to create for is to choose demographics or even psychographics over living, breathing human beings. Quiet Power Strategy requires you to find your muse: a real person you can really create for. Don't know someone who needs What You Want to Create? Find someone who does. This is a non-negotiable aspect of business strategy.

Ideally, you'll have a Virtual Focus Group of about 5 people whom you can observe, reference, and design for. I call this a "Virtual" Focus Group because you do not need to get these people behind a two-way mirror and show them two different versions of your widget to determine which they prefer. Instead, you can virtually observe the members of your focus group on social platforms like Facebook, Pinterest,

Instagram, or LinkedIn and learn their behaviors, beliefs, and needs. Using that information, you can then discern how you'll create something perfect for them, connect with them in a way that's both authentic for you and meaningful to them, and sell to them in a way that's effective and easy for everyone.

You'll consider the needs of Who You Want to Create For as you decide What You Want to Create. Examine what these people really value in terms of details. For some people, price is always a determining factor in what they buy. For others, it's design. Still others prefer convenience, consistency, or luxury service. Think about how the people you've chosen to create for like to buy and what makes them choose one solution over another. This will guide you as you approach your strategy for What You Want to Create.

You would have a much harder time selling luxury amenities to a price-conscious market than to people who expect their every whim to be met. Likewise, it would be easier to sell convenient but design-focused products to a market that prefers Target than to sell them inexpensive products with outdated style. Don't overlook this important strategic step; it can be the difference between a business that faces friction in the market and a business that gains easy traction.

How They Respond

The way you track your business is by the way customers respond. You need to know what kind of responses inspire you, what kind of responses your customers are most likely to make, and what kind of responses move the needle on your business. When those things are all different, your business is in trouble. When you can devise a strategic approach that allows each category of response to line up, you've got traction.

Begin to plot this part of your strategy by considering what kinds of responses really inspire you in your business. Sales are just one way you can track the response you receive to what your business is doing, and it might not be the thing that keeps you moving on a daily basis. Do you feel jazzed every time the Facebook share count goes up? Do you love getting thoughtful questions from people engaging with your work? Do you cheer every time a client refers your services?

Next, consider how your potential customers are most likely to respond to what you're creating and how you're connecting with them. Some groups of customers are extremely vocal and will respond with unchecked enthusiasm for what you're doing. Other groups are much more private and their responses are much more subtle. Think critically about how your customers naturally respond so that you can design tracking metrics that will tell you when your marketing or sales efforts are effective.

Finally, consider what responses create growth in your business. All businesses thrive on sales, but every business has different ways of getting to a sale. When you know what responses lead to sales and how you can track them, then you can focus on actions that lead to those responses. Instead of seeing a sea of options, you have a precise set of criteria for evaluating what's in front of you.

In my own business, we run a membership site called Kick Start Labs. In addition to tracking sign-ups for the community, another response we track is longevity. How long do people stay involved with the community and continue to pay the monthly fee? One thing that leads to longevity is the engagement of the overall community, so we track how many new conversations are started every week in our forum. The more engaged the overall community is, the more likely people are to stick around and continue to pay the monthly fee.

Maybe you know that referrals from existing customers lead to a higher rate of sales. So you decide to encourage referrals and track how often a new customer comes from an existing customer. Maybe you know that completing one program with your business leads to an exponentially higher rate of sales on your second-tier program, so you make changes to your first program so that it's easier for customers to finish, then track the improvement in completion rates. When you know what responses from prospects and customers help get the results you want in your business, you can focus your actions to get more of those responses.

Iterative Strategic Planning

I encourage you to approach your Quiet Power Strategic Plan iteratively. Remember that What You Want to Create influences Who You Want to Create For and How You Want to Connect With Others influences How They Respond. Every choice creates new opportunities and closes the door on others in every part of your plan. This is natural and a necessary part of creating a strategic plan.

With each iteration of your plan make choices that get your business closer to your vision. Look to make choices that support other parts of your plan and make tactical actions more aligned with what feels easeful. As I mentioned earlier, don't try to get your plan right the first time. Start with the part that feels most certain to you. For some that will be How You Want to Connect, for others it might be What You Want to Create, and for still others it could be Who You Want to Create For. Make a few choices, take a few directions, and then work on other parts of the plan, adding definition and precision as you go.

Be sure to check with yourself at each section to make sure you're tapping in to your Quiet Power and not relying on the "shoulds" that have been directing your business to this point. If you'd like further support, you can download my corresponding Quiet Power Strategy™ Map at taragentile.com/quietpower

PART THREE: PROMPTS

In this final section of this book, you'll find prompts and directives that help keep my clients and me focused on our own Quiet Power Strategies. Feel free to use these ideas as a way to direct your focus back to your own strategy or when you're feeling a bit stumped with your direction. Remember to always make perception, discernment, and focus a part of your daily work routine.

Perception Lends Perspective

Being stuck in the weeds of your business has an exceptionally strong correlation to being stuck in your own head. Instead of looking to what the outside world might have to offer, you try to think your way out of every situation or question. Your customers, however, aren't in your head; they're out in their local communities and online neighborhoods. The path you need to walk to lead yourself to your big goals isn't in your head, either.

Every step you need to take is outside, and the only way to discern those next steps is to begin by perceiving the opportunities, obstacles, information, and possibilities that exist outside your skull. While much of your Quiet Power comes from within, the key to leveraging it starts without. When you get clear on what's really happening around you, you'll know what to create, who to engage, and how to show up in the market.

When you use your powers of perception to get the perspective you need to make better decisions and discern your next steps, each step forward takes less energy. You don't have to push as much because being more aware of what's going on around you means being more aware of what's going to be most effective for you.

You can leverage perception in every area of your business to gain more perspective. One of the easiest changes in perception you can make is in the energy you put into social media. Social media has largely been touted as a great new way to reach customers in the Social Era. That's true. But most people interpret that to mean that social media is a great way to broadcast your message (read: your self-promotional message) to your potential customers.

However, the power of social media isn't in the broadcasting; it's in the listening. Instead of focusing on how many messages you should be sending out via Twitter or your Facebook page, consider how many new insights you can gather each day by listening more. Social media is a wealth of social data: the things people say about their problems or pain points, the things people do to try to rectify them, the things people feel about what they're trying to accomplish.

When you listen closely, you might only make one or two broadcasts, but those broadcasts are going to be exponentially more effective than if you're only worried about broadcasting. Your message can be crafted to cut through the Noise and be received by exactly the people who need to hear it. Your Quiet Power will make it easier to connect and, in turn, to know what to create.

When you're focused on broadcasting, you're going to be always thinking about broadcasting. When you're listening, you only need to respond. It's just like when you're sitting across from a friend at a coffee shop; it's a back and forth. Focusing on perception gives you the perspective of a natural conversation that makes what you're trying to do easier, more natural. It's not something new you need to learn or a tactic you have to master; instead, it's unlearning the habit of overthinking.

Connections are the Gold Standard

There's a reason the "World Wide Web" took off: we crave connection. Over the 20th century, we gradually got more and more disconnected from our daily lives. We were disconnected from our families, our governments, our food sources, and our own ideas–among many other things. Quiet Power people work hard to mend those connections because connections are the gold standard today. Who you know, how you're connected to the people who can help you get to the next step, and what ideas you're connecting can largely pay your tolls on the information superhighway.

Part of leveraging your Quiet Power is finding new opportunities to make connections. You might connect two people you truly adore, or you might connect a pain point with a brand-new insight. You will definitely build a team of cheerleaders, collaborators, and co-conspirators. The key to discovering the power you already possess in networking and connecting with people is understanding why you're such a great person to connect with in the first place.

Brigitte Lyons, the founder of B: The Forward-Thinking PR Agency and one of my own co-conspirators, says the reason we get nervous about connecting with others is that we think of networking as a process of extracting value from someone else. As long as we're in that mindset, most of us will try to just extract the value from ourselves instead of connecting: we'll attempt to learn new skills, power through draining tasks, and settle for mediocre results.

That's how we get in trouble. We try to build a business in a bubble, even when business today is about connection by definition. In the Social Era, work doesn't look like it used to. Value doesn't even look like it used to. Instead, work and value creation happen in and through the network. Co-creation is standard, relationship is capital, innovation is vocation. Working "solo" is possible only because we're working together—and because we have new ways of working together.

Quiet Power Strategy asks us to get creative with how we meet people, connect with them, and, ultimately, work with them. There are so many ways to both contribute to and receive value from the connections you make. Consider what you're coming to the connection with: your skills, your strengths, your know-how. You have so much to give.

If you view the nurturing of personal connections as an opportunity for generosity, you're much more likely to build more valuable connections for yourself. Of course, I don't mean letting yourself get steamrolled by other people's needs. It's not about giving until you don't have anything more to give; it's about showing up as your genuine, generous self. It's also about being open to the opportunities that real connection can create.

Ideas work the same way. Quiet Power people connect ideas as readily as they connect people. And they do so in the spirit of possibility and opportunity, not greed. Look for originality, look for innovation. Don't force it, perceive it. It's already all around you.

Spend part of every day connecting things. Small and large. Narrow and wide. See what happens.

Discernment

Personalize, Don't Generalize

I hear it all the time: "Tara, I have no problem talking to or selling to clients on the phone or in person, but the moment I sit down to write some sales copy, or my bio, or a blog post, I freeze." There's a very good reason this happens: we're social creatures. It's a fact of both biological and psychological human nature. When you try to communicate without the context of a social experience, it becomes exponentially more difficult.

Unfortunately, we're faced with tasks on a daily basis–such as writing–that seem to be disconnected from the social experience. Not only that, our social makeup prefers an intimate experience. It's much harder to engage a large group of people than it is to engage an individual. Smart copywriters, product development specialists, marketers, and speakers know to focus first on the individual and then engage a group one person at a time. They personalize, they don't generalize.

When we generalize, we miss a lot of details. Those details are often the secret to unlocking a new level of creativity and effectiveness in product development, messaging, and sales. To boot, your customers don't want to align with generalizations. They want to feel like what your business has created was made especially for them. While mass solutions may have had traction in the industrial era, the Social Era demands a new level of attention to detail and specialization. By beginning with a real person who has real needs that your skills, talents, and passion make you uniquely equipped to serve or create for, you don't miss the details. You see her experience, you understand her process, and you discover both acute and deep needs.

While traditionally scale has required making products or services less personal, by starting with even a single personalization, you can create products, marketing, and conversation that feel orders of magnitude more profound for the right people. Your business can scale based on intimacy and precise understanding instead of casting a wider net and hoping to get by. You can make each transaction feel personal.

We're better at relating to people than we are to demographics. As a result, if you work hard to understand the needs, desires, and frustrations of that one person who brings your genius to life, you'll get better results. You create, write, develop, or code just for that muse. Then, you discover there are thousands out there just like him or her. So when you focus on The One, you're really creating for a whole world of people who relate to your own Quiet Power.

Make personalization your mantra. Repeat it every time you start to feel stuck. It will help you rethink problems and innovate on old ideas. It will help you find new ways around convention and help you create things that more people go crazy for.

After all, "Personalize, don't generalize" is why I'm writing this book to you.

Discernment

Choose How You're Perceived

Dr. Phil McGraw says, "You teach people how to treat you." This is true in your personal life, but it's never more true than in business. You are a brand. You are your brand. How you communicate your brand, its story, its values, its modus operandi, determines how others will interact with you.

Just as in teaching others how to treat you, you can teach them how to perceive your business. Do you want your brand name to be mentioned alongside your heroes in the industry? Do you want your business to be perceived as the steadfast option in an industry full of flakes? Do you want your brand to be the warm, friendly alternative to the colder default option?

Every choice you make is an opportunity to choose how your business is perceived. In my own work with clients, what I see is both abnegation of that privilege and panic in the face of what they perceive as the market dictating how they are perceived. Let me share an example.

Back when Etsy, the online marketplace for handmade and small batch goods, was just leaving the startup phase, they brought me in to deliver talks and seller consulting on pricing and the effects of pricing strategy on small batch goods. I would share how you need to make sure the price you're asking for your product actually covers the full cost of what it takes to make it, pays you much better than minimum wage for the time you spend making it, and pays you a profit, even at wholesale.

Inevitably, Etsy sellers would ask how they could justify such a price when so many other sellers were selling their goods for considerably less. They were allowing the artificially low prices within the Etsy marketplace to influence their behavior, while that behavior in turn influenced how their products were perceived. How do you react when you see a price that feels too good to be true? I react by assuming that there is something wrong with the product, and maybe you do too.

Having an artificially low price to compete with the rest of the Etsy market was potentially creating bigger problems for these makers and designers. They were giving the impression that their product was possibly flawed, shoddy, or inadequate. That perception wasn't helping sales, even if on paper they were now competing with the rest of the market. By raising their prices, there was a good chance they could stand out, represent their products accurately, and earn a better perception within the market.

Perception is reality, as the adage goes. If a part of your story gives people an impression that your work is shoddy, then your work is shoddy. If the whole of your story gives people an impression that you have museum-quality work, then your work belongs in a museum. That begs the question, how do you ensure that your business is being perceived the way you want it to be perceived?

Of course, you must start with a process of discernment. You have to know exactly how the way you want others to perceive your business ties in to who you are, what you want, and the experiences you want to create for your customers, so that you can lead with that information. Sally Hogshead,

New York Times bestselling author of *How the World Sees You* and creator of the Fascination Advantage system, calls this "front-loading your value." You can prime the pump with the way you want others to perceive your business and the value it provides. When you can clearly articulate your unique positioning and what you deliver at your highest value, you set the stage for being perceived the way you want to be perceived. Others can't dictate your story because you've so clearly told the story yourself.

The best way to tell that story is through a careful consideration of the details. Your details might include visual assets, narrative assets, your products, your services, your pricing, the media you've been featured in, the customers you serve, or the language you use. Each detail is just another chance to teach others how to perceive you.

High-end bohemian lifestyle brand Anthropologie does this expertly. Every detail of their customer experience is geared to put them at the top of the market. The products themselves, the prices, the way each garment is photographed, the design of each store, and the paper the catalogs are printed on all speak to the story they're telling and the perception they want to have among their customers. It's a carefully curated set of details that add up to a big picture that conveys the image they want to have.

In your own business, are there places where the details of your brand are less than clear? Less than consistent? Do you know how you want your business to be perceived and how that perception relates back to who you are, what you want, and the experiences you want to create for your customers? Be proactive about the image and story you put out into the world. Above all, choose the story for yourself, because businesses that thrive are willing to let their unique voice sing out above the noise of the marketplace.

Discernment

Take Credit

Results make you radiate. Your business is helping to create noticeable change for your clients and customers. It doesn't help you to be humble about it. Humility may be a virtue, and it might even pay some dividends in your business, but that doesn't mean you have to disown your success. Quiet Power people combine a healthy dose of gratitude for the wherewithal of their customers with a strong sense of their own professional achievement. Do the same and you'll glow.

That radiant glow is what's attractive about you and your business. You don't need to shout about your achievements; just accept them and the power they lend you. Tell stories, create beautiful work, fix problems, make your customers' hopes and dreams come true. It's not about you; it's about what you do for others.

Seth Godin is a master of radiant self-promotion. He tells stories that highlight results. He communicates with substance. He proves that "taking credit" is just another way of saying "showing up." But he's not just good at self-promotion; he knows what will be most effective and why. He writes, "Nobody says, 'That Yo Yo Ma, he's so self-promotional,' or, 'Can you believe what a self-promoter the Dalai Lama is?' That's because they're not promoting themselves. They're promoting useful ideas. They're promoting tactics or products that actually benefit the person they're reaching out to."

They show up. They take credit. And they do it for you. All the masterful self-promoters take credit because it's in your best interest. They create for you, they hustle for you, they get results for you. Selfish self-promotion falls flat. Compassionate self-promotion is engaging.

Are you allowing yourself to glow? Are you showing up and delivering on what you promise? Are you focused on why taking credit for the work you do matters to others? Take some time to discern what stories you can tell and where you can show up to take credit for what you do for others. Own it.

Discernment

Get Help

When Brigitte Lyons quit her high-powered PR agency job to pursue an independent career at the intersection of entrepreneurship and media, she started out trying to teach entrepreneurs how to do their own public relations and media outreach. She blogged, developed programs, and networked with movers and shakers. Eventually, we started doing business together on my business coaching program.

In working more and more with the business owners she really wanted to reach, it became clear that they just didn't have the time to learn how to do things for themselves. They wanted help. They were desperate for it and willing to pay.

Brigitte knew herself enough to realize she didn't want to be enveloping pitches and talking on the phone with journalists all day long. She was interested in working closely with entrepreneurs but wanted to focus on strategy, not implementation. Brigitte called me one day and said, "I need a Maggie."

An intern Brigitte had worked with in her agency days, Maggie was an expert implementer and brilliant publicist. She knew how to work pitches and editors. She could get placements through a combination of shrewd execution and fabulous connections. A Maggie could help Brigitte do the work she loved while giving her clients what they needed.

Just days later, Maggie emailed Brigitte. She was looking for a new position and wondered if Brigitte had any connections. Brigitte acted immediately with a proposal: get in on the ground level of a brand-new agency and only work with clients she'd love. After some hard negotiations, Maggie was on board. Brigitte now had an agency through which she could deliver the value her clients were after and someone to do the work she really didn't want to do.

Brigitte got help. She could have tried to do it all herself. She'd have had no one to blame but herself if she missed an opportunity or didn't come through for a client. But she took the risk to bring someone else on to her team. I've worked with entrepreneurs who have always only done it themselves and entrepreneurs in charge of sizable teams who have worked hard to maintain control over every aspect of their idea. Ultimately, the underlying problem is the same: we want responsibility for our own outcomes. On the surface, it might look like an epidemic of wanting all the praise. But dig deeper and the bigger motivator seems to be wanting to have only ourselves to point the finger at for inevitable failure.

People who leverage Quiet Power fight their natural tendency to want only themselves to blame if things go wrong. They beat back the voices that urge them to go it on their own and not get others involved. This aspect of self-leadership is really self-control. It takes self-control to not keep working another hour, to not learn a new skill you have no business learning, to not make a plan that feeds most of the decision-making back to you.

It's also self-control, not busyness, that keeps you in business. You can work until you're blue in the face and still not succeed. That's not to say that hard work doesn't or won't pay off. But is what you're spending your day doing really getting you one step (or better, a few steps) ahead? Are your daily actions tuned to the goal you've set in front of you? Your goal can't be to work yourself to the bone. The sense of accomplishment you've been missing won't come from just checking tasks off a list. What you're missing is progress, the sense that what you're doing matters in the larger scheme of things.

Getting help can keep you moving forward. Few dreams are realized from the blood, sweat, and tears of one visionary. Instead, they're collective efforts. They draw on the expertise and Quiet Power of the people enlisted to get the job done. Brigitte's dream required Maggie's Quiet Power to be realized. And together, they're able to create something even better. Today, they're aiming to work with non-profit organizations that are interested in progressive, cutting-edge media and outreach strategy. This is something Brigitte would have never created on her own. But by asking for help, not only could she relax and enjoy her work a little more, she was actually able to conceive of something better than her original dream.

What's more, Brigitte has a whole team of people around her to celebrate when she succeeds, and their collective effort means the agency's victories are a collective win. And when those inevitable failures occur, as convenient as it would be to know it's her fault something has gone wrong, it's even more convenient for Brigitte to have a team to reinvent, pivot, and plow ahead with.

If your dreams always feel just a bit out of reach, it might be because you need help reaching. If you feel overwhelmed by the prospect of actually bringing your vision to fruition, it might be because you need to enlist help.

Focus

Be Consistent

Chris Guillebeau was simultaneously hard at work at what would become a *New York Times* bestselling book, *The $100 Startup*, and finishing his goal of visiting every country on the planet before the age of 35. Guillebeau always has a lot of irons in the fire. His micropublishing business, Unconventional Guides, has released information products on everything from travel hacking to freelance writing to creating a business empire to turning your creativity into a career. He produces an incredibly in-demand conference each year called the World Domination Summit. His last book was about people who pursue big projects or goals in order to find happiness.

You could look at Chris's world and see a bunch of disparate projects. You could wonder what travel hacking has to do with writing or business. But once inside Chris's community, you see how everything is tied together. Chris always poses the question, "How do you live a remarkable life in a conventional world?" at the beginning of every World

Domination Summit. That question could well be the main theme of the community he's built for thousands of people.

You would not be mistaken to also see impeccable attention to detail, striving for excellence, or innovative solutions to old problems as themes of his work. Chris's Quiet Power comes largely from consistency. Whatever he does, you know how he's going to do it; it will be unconventional, remarkable, and innovative.

Consistency is a matter of focus, and being focused doesn't mean eschewing variety. When you know the thread that binds your work together, you can explore a lot of territory with intense focus and not throw off the people who buy your products or engage your services. Pamela Slim, author of Body of Work: Finding the Thread That Ties Your Story Together, writes, "Consistent impact over the course of your life on a body of work you care about deeply is legacy." Quiet Power Strategy and legacy have much in common. In fact, you could say that legacy is the what and Quiet Power Strategy is the how.

If you look at what you're creating, the ideas you're exploring, and the choices you're making as details within a larger story, the imperative of consistency becomes an easier pill to swallow. Instead of limiting yourself, you get the opportunity to play with your ideas and choices so that they become consistent with the legacy you want to build. You can look for a novel way to approach that crazy idea you had in the shower so that it plays a part in the story you're telling about who you are, what you want, and the experiences you want to create for others.

Go further, and the details become more precise. Consistency can be about word choice, visual representation, design choices, pricing, and content that adds up to an authentic representation of your business or work. Being consistent doesn't always mean making things look or sound the same, but it does mean making them feel the same. It's like how Stephen King can write books with vastly different settings, plots, tropes, and characters and still give you that sense of uneasiness, that sense of coming unhinged, that you associate with his work.

Quiet Power people rely on details to help tell their stories bit by bit over time. They look for every opportunity to maximize the power of what they're doing by reinforcing the right message with the right details. They know details speak louder than words and they work to get them right. Having the "right" details, of course, is not about having the same details as everyone else. Having the right details means making the choices that add up to an authentic representation of you and your business.

Those details must be consistent because it's not an individual detail that tells the story but the consistent execution and application of those details.

Take a look through your world. Consider everything from your wardrobe to your online presence to the way you introduce yourself at events. Examine your approach to sales conversations, your conversations with colleagues, and your choice of projects. Is there a consistent thread that ties these things together? Take that thread and leverage it to create a more consistent experience of you and the work you do. That consistent thread is a key source of your power, and it's found in quiet details that could easily go overlooked.

Invest In Your Unique Point of View

I met my partner, Sean, on OKCupid. It might have been love at first sight, but because I was skeptical of falling in love with an online dating profile, I certainly didn't recognize it at the start.

"I make better kimchi than your Korean grandmother," his profile said. I was immediately intrigued, not because I have any great love of kimchi but because that was how he chose to describe himself. He also went on to list knitting, literary science fiction, and jazz among his interests. Honestly, I thought he was too good to be true. I thought someone was messing with me. I closed my laptop on his profile and made a mental note to message him later.

That same night, not more than 30 minutes later, I bumped into him in town. It turns out the friend I was with was also an acquaintance of Sean's. They said a quick hello and parted ways. Sean politely—and I'm always certain to use the word "politely" when I tell this story because it was exactly that way, so polite and so very "him"–came back to introduce himself and then went about his business. He was real. He appeared to be exactly as he portrayed himself online, part mountain man from Montana by way of Alaska and part lover of fine things and good food.

We went on our first date a week later. Not surprisingly, conversation was easy and flowed through two glasses of wine. When I mentioned my great love of Star Trek, Sean said, "Oh! I have something I have to show you, then" and went for his backpack. He pulled out his wallet, opened it with a grin, and showed me the first plastic sleeve, in which he had placed a cutout of Kirk and Spock from a Star Trek comic. That was it. Looking back on that night, we both have pinpointed that moment as the moment we knew–even if it took us a few days or weeks to really come to terms with the surprise that we had finally found that person who could really be our true partner.

Now, why this revelation of my romantic history in a book about business and strategy? Because it was Sean's Quiet Power that I fell in love with and continue to love every day. A less powerful person wouldn't have revealed the geekery contained in his wallet on a first date. A less powerful person wouldn't have even brought up Star Trek to begin with. A less powerful person would have missed the opportunity of a lifetime by hiding her unique point of view.

A couple of weeks after we began dating, Sean dropped off a jar of kimchi and some soup at my apartment. I promptly ate the soup. The kimchi I put in the cabinet. No way was I going to eat that.

A few months later, going through my cabinets in an attempt to find some movie snacks, he discovered the jar of kimchi. "Um, this wasn't sealed. It needed to be in the refrigerator," he said.

What happened next completely shocked this suburban girl

who grew up on processed food and suburban chain restaurants: He opened the jar and popped a big bite of fermented (and, I assumed, spoiled) cabbage in his mouth. Then, he plucked out a bite of sour, spicy kimchi for me. Blinded by love and inspired by his enthusiasm, I ate it.

It was good.

Many months later, he told me he'd slept poorly because he had read too much stimulating information before he went to sleep; The Art of Fermentation was lying open on the floor next to the bed. He'd spent many restless hours considering new ideas for pickled vegetables. Then on New Year's Eve, he dropped off a jar of kimchi to the newest chef in town, and a well-decorated one at that. New Year's Day, he told me how he brought in another jar for his coworkers to try. He said, "I just want everyone to know how good this stuff is. I love it and I want them to love it too."

Sean invests precious time, energy, and money in what he loves and ensuring others can love it, too. He doesn't worry that people might turn up their nose at a food that has been historically prepared by burying it in the ground. He doesn't hide his obsession or waste an opportunity to tell people about his latest experiment. He is fully invested in his unique point of view.

His friends, family, customers, and coworkers hold him in high esteem because of this. I am incredibly proud to be with him. You never get the sense he is working a script (even when he is) or manipulating a conversation to his advantage (even when he does). His strategy is always authentic, aligned, and true to who he is and what he wants. He's always mindful of how his unique point of view creates experiences for others.

You see, it's not that working a script or manipulating the course of conversation is bad. It's not. We do it on a daily basis. Daniel Pink writes in To Sell Is Human, "The ability to move others to exchange what they have for what we have is crucial to our survival and our happiness." We all find ourselves in the position of having to convince, move, and sell others regularly, regardless of whether sales is in our job description. And because sales, or even persuasion, is often a matter we would like to avoid, we co-opt others' formulas, tactics, and points of view as our own in order to avoid putting our true ideas on the line.

When you own—invest in, even—your unique point of view, you become more persuasive, more relatable, and more compelling. When you don't try to ignore the quirks and fascinating tidbits that make you you, those kinds of conversation become not only fun, but more effective. Sure, your quirks may not make for mainstream success, but the truth is that mainstream success is all but dead. Even "big stars" are carried by niche audiences. Your goal isn't to sound like everyone else; your goal is to sound like you. Your Quiet Power Strategy must be rooted in all the idiosyncratic and unconventional aspects of your point of view.

More than that, you should invest in them, literally. Take the time, energy, and money that's needed to explore your unique makeup. If you're into Star Trek, go to a convention. If you're into fermented foods, fill up your cabinets with them. If you're into literature, invest in subscriptions to your favorite journals. This is not a matter to approach with frugality. Watch your Quiet Power balance go up with each investment.

We all come from different places, have different opinions, and see things different ways. People who leverage Quiet Power lean into those differences.

They invest energy, time, and relationships into making their unique points of view the center of their businesses. Instead of singing the same song as everyone else, they sing a song that's all their own.

They don't worry about being weird or contrary. They embrace it.

They might not have as many fans as the of-the-moment brand, but they do have longevity with all the right people. And there's nothing more powerful than that.

Focus

Communicate Strength

Society has long equated "quiet" with "meek." But in my experience, quiet people don't lack opinions or ideas. They don't lack experience or even confidence. They're not wishy-washy, and they're not shy. Being quiet doesn't mean you're a pushover. Instead, "quiet" can be finding comfort and peace in your mastery, self-leadership, and intentional restraint.

Quiet Power Strategy redefines "quiet" as an inner sense of knowing that drives us to success on our own terms. It's calm, focused, and determined. It doesn't need to shout because it trusts in its ability to actively connect with the right people for the right reasons. "Quiet" doesn't wait. It makes the right things happen at the right time.

At the heart of taking comfort in your Quiet is the ability to communicate strength outwardly. It's not enough to have that inner knowing; you have to share to get more people on board with your message, product, or organization. You have to stand firm, not hedge, and keep your mouth shut when you're anything less than ready to go big.

Howard Schultz, the CEO of Starbucks—the man who made

Starbucks the brand you now know and not just some Seattle store selling coffee beans—embodies the idea of communicating strength. His goal has always been to have Starbucks stores speak for themselves. For over 2 decades, the company didn't advertise on television. Instead, they let their baristas, customers, and reputation fill stores and queue up drive-thrus.

He wrote in his first book, *Pour Your Heart* into It, "To stay vigorous, a company needs to provide a stimulating and challenging environment for all these types: the dreamer, the entrepreneur, the professional manager, and the leader. If it doesn't, it risks becoming yet another mediocre corporation." That kind of environment doesn't just attract and keep great employees, it attracts loyal customers who spread the message of the brand and strategic partners who see the potential of a business beyond even what its creators see. Creating a stimulating and challenging environment is largely a product of communicating strength. When a leader or a brand puts out a message with confidence, it immediately becomes more appealing.

But what does this look like in practice? It starts with taking yourself seriously. I doubt that Schultz wallowed in the kind of self-indulgent doubt that keeps so many smart, creative people from starting or growing their businesses. He pitched his ideas with strength, he made tough decisions based on personal conviction, and he garnered support as he made changes. To this day, he maintains focus on both his personal and professional mission and actively steers his company in that direction.

While you're perceiving, discerning, and focusing on your work, you have a duty to communicate (with) strength. The thing is that you can get caught up in all the observation and forget to make yourself heard.

The work you do deserves an audience. It deserves a strong voice. State your opinions clearly and without qualification. Speak directly to the people who are listening to you.

Don't hedge. Express. Articulate.

Leave room for expansion but not for equivocation.

Know Where You're Headed

When you start any new venture, you expect to pivot. You make both large and small course corrections based on what you see in front of you, what's working, and what's not. You have an idea of where you'd like to end up or what you'd like to create, but decisions are largely based on "what's now" as opposed to "what's to come."

But there comes a point where that kind of approach no longer serves you. Quiet Power Strategy demands a more future-focused view of your venture. In order to focus ruthlessly, you need to know where you're headed.

A side benefit of this is that when you know where you're headed, your customers and prospects feel more at ease. They're not continually surprised by the products you release or the marketing campaigns you unleash. They feel comfortable, empowered, and assured. And it's probably not a surprise to you that people who are comfortable, empowered, and assured are much more likely to buy from you.

Knowing where you're headed requires you to make some decisions. You need to discern a destination based on

What You Want to Create and How You Want to Connect with people. Once you know the destination, you can plot your course.

Almost three years ago, I set off on a cross-country road trip—just me and my 4-year-old daughter. I was headed to Astoria, Oregon, which was to be my new home. I'd never done a road trip of that magnitude before, but it seemed straightforward. If I drove approximately 600 miles a day, I would make it in 8 days. There were some landmarks I wanted to hit: Millennium Park in Chicago, The Mall of America in Minneapolis, and Mt. Rushmore in South Dakota. I figured we'd find plenty of other cool stuff to see along the way.

I had a rough idea of where I wanted to end up each night but knew it would be a fool's errand to try to book hotels ahead of time. I chose to stick with one hotel chain, the Hampton Inn, and find the closest one to wherever we were going when we made a pitstop for lunch each day. With the exception of a gnarly detour between Minnesota and South Dakota, the trip was completely smooth sailing. Later, when I told my coach about it, I said, "I got really lucky."

She replied, "No, you didn't. You don't believe in luck." How true she was. She continued, "You made a plan and followed it. It was just the right amount of knowing where you were headed and being open to possibility. You made that trip as smooth as it was." I left the conversation that day with a new mantra, "I created this." It's a useful phrase every time you feel yourself tempted to allow luck to take credit for your accomplishments.

Luck doesn't have much sway in my world. I choose destinations, make navigational plans, take detours when I choose or when necessary, and end up where I wanted to go in the first place. When I consider what goes wrong for others, it's not the "making plans" part; it's the choice of destination. In other words, they have no idea where they're headed.

Quiet Power people start with where they're headed and

then discern a rough idea of what it's going to take to get there. They reverse engineer the success they want—they don't chase after other people's success. Quiet Power people also apply this particular strategy on both the macro level and the micro level. They know where their business is headed, but they also know where any marketing campaign, strategic relationship, or sales conversation is headed and discern the necessary steps from there.

They stay on task, on target, and super productive because they know where they're going. Do you?

Focus

Rest

Resting is an underutilized strategy. The problem is that we have a tendency to fill time with tasks instead of waiting to see our plans come to fruition on their own. The road from follow-your-passion to thriving business can be a bumpy one. Once you realize "if you build it, they will come" isn't a business strategy, it's tempting to spend every waking hour tweaking, writing, emailing, networking, and trying to push through.

"While you're doing it, doing it, doing it," Michael Gerber writes in *The E-Myth Revisited*, "there's something much more important that isn't getting done." The fact of the matter is this: busyness isn't business. Don't confuse the two.

Taking a break doesn't mean you're not making progress; it means that you've created the conditions, systems, and plan that work without your constant attention. That should be the goal of any creator, entrepreneur, or business owner.

When you make busywork for yourself, you take your focus off of what really counts. Check your to-do list against your strategic plan and learn to call it quits when there is nothing left to do to move your mission forward.

Busying yourself doesn't level the learning curve. Being busy doesn't create ease. Being busy doesn't create satisfaction. Know where you want to go and create a plan to get there. Remove any and all unnecessary tasks and busy work. Take time off, explore, enjoy. Have faith that your plan will take time and that doesn't mean that you have to fill it with work that is meaningless.

Make time to rest. To recharge. To savor.

Conclusion

Quiet Power Strategy is both a practice you use in your business and a state of mind that transforms the way you work. When you start to perceive your business as a set of choices that work together to create value, impact your customers, and stake your position in the market, you'll see more and more choices in front of you. But instead of that nervous, overwhelmed feeling you get when you come across choices now, you'll have a strategic plan that allows you to approach your options with confident discernment.

Your business has suffered too long while you've been wandering in the weeds. This is the time to find within you the self-leadership you need to guide your business to the vision you have for it. You can take the helm and steer yourself and your business to the results you want. You can discern your next steps. You can focus on a plan of action that makes business growth feel easeful.

I encourage you to see your daily life as an opportunity to practice your Quiet Power Strategy and leverage the ways you're most effective. I invite you to reject the "shoulds" and "musts" and focus on what works for you. Finally, I ask you to set aside time every day to find your Quiet in this Noisy world. If you take nothing else from this book, it should be a strategic framework for finding the peace that allows you to do your business your way day in and day out.

The Exercises

5 Key Questions for Uncovering Your Quiet Power Strategy

- What is your vision for making life meaningfully better for your audience, clients, or customers and how will you measure your success?

- What conversation is your business a part of and what voices in that conversation are your best prospects looking for an alternative to?

- What will you use to represent your unique point of view to engage customers who are excited about your business's strengths, skills, and passion?

- How will you further invest in your unique point of view to attract your best prospects?

- What product, marketing, sales, and management systems can you put in place to support and enhance your business's unique point of view?

Declare Your Chief Initiative

- What singular goal (Chief Initiative) will you pursue for the next 6-12 months that will keep you motivated and inspired about your business?

- What conditions will exist in your business when you achieve that goal?

- What sub-goals need to be achieved to make your Chief Initiative more likely to be realized?

- What systems need to be put in place to realize those sub-goals?

- How can you involve your team to drive your business in the direction of the Chief Initiative?

Quiet Power Strategic Plan Warm-Up

- When have you felt most persuasive? What conditions do you need to be more persuasive? What actions help you make your case?

- What personal values or principles influence the way you approach your work and business? How do those values or principles help differentiate your business from the rest of the market?

- What conditions make it easiest for you to meet new people?

- How do you like people to respond to you or your ideas? What responses motivate and inspire you?

- What does success look like for you and your business? What does success look like for your customers?

Quiet Power Strategic Plan

What You Want to Create

- What need do you want to fill?

- What conversation is your business a part of?

- What's Your Vision?

- How does What You Want to Create differentiate your business from the rest of the market?

How You Want to Connect

- What is a natural way for you to connect with other people?

- What personal values guide your relationships?

- What's your unique point of view?

- How does How You Want to Connect differentiate your business from the rest of the market?

Who You Want to Create For

- List 5 specific people you want to create for (Virtual Focus Group).

- What's most important to these people? What really matters to them?

How They Respond

- How are they most likely to respond to what you create? What actions feel most natural to them?

- How will you channel those actions into the results you want for your business?

Appendix II

Recommend Resources

Chapter 1

Generative advantage: Haque, Umair. *Betterness: Economics for Humans.* Boston, Mass.: Harvard Business Review, 2011. Kindle.

Don't waste your energy: Fey, Tina. *Bossypants.* New York: Little, Brown, 2011. Print.

Chapter 2

Impostor Complex: Geisler, Tanya. "12 Lies of the Impostor Complex (and One Truth)." *Tanya Geisler Step into Your Starring Role.* 2014. Web. 1 Dec. 2014. (**http://tanyageisler.com**)

Onlyness: Merchant, Nilofer. *11 Rules for Creating Value in the #Social Era.* Nilofer Merchant, 2012. Kindle.

More potential for growth: Rath, Tom, and Marcus Buckingham. *StrengthsFinder 2.0*. New York: Gallup, 2007. Print.

Natural ways you communicate: Hogshead, Sally. How The World Sees You: Discover Your Highest Value Through the Science of Fascination. New York: HarperBusiness, 2014. Print.

Chapter 3

Integrated set of choices: Lafley, A. G., and Roger L. Martin. *Playing to Win: How Strategy Really Works*. Boston, MA: Harvard Business Review, 2013. Kindle.

Markets are conversations: Levine, Rick, Christopher Locke, Doc Searls, David Weinberger, Jack McKee, J.P. Rangaswami, and Dan Gillmor. *The Cluetrain Manifesto: The End of Business as Usual*. Basic, 2011. Kindle. Anniversary Edition

Chapter 4

Playing big: Mohr, Tara. *Playing Big: Find Your Voice, Your Mission, Your Message.* New York: Gotham, 2014. Print.

Get out of the building: Blank, Steve. *Steve Blank | Entrepreneurship and Conversation*. Web. (**http://steveblank.com**)

Five whys: Ries, Eric. *The Lean Startup: How Today's Entrepreneurs Use Continuous Innovation to Create Radically Successful Businesses.* New York: Crown Business, 2011. Kindle.

Chapter 5

Powerful choice: LaPorte, Danielle. *The Desire Map Daily: A Guide to*

Feeling Your Power Everyday. SoundsTrue, 2014. Audio.

Somatic psychology: Bernstein, Dr. Susan. *The Sensational Shift*. Web. (**http://sensationalshift.com**)

Tap into intuition: Selingo, Tracey. *Woo School*. Web. (**http://wooschool.com**)

Chapter 6

Busyness: Kreider, Tim. "The 'Busy' Trap." *New York Times: Opinionator.* June 30, 2012. Web.

To be bored: Haque, Umair. "The Bullshit Machine." *Medium: Bad Words.* July 16, 2014. Web.

Chapter 7

Louis CK: Zinoman, Jason. "A Softer Side of Loathing: Louis CK Performs at Madison Square Garden." *New York Times: Arts*. January 8, 2015. Web.

Killer product: Weinberg, Gabriel R., and Justin Mares. *Traction: A Startup Guide to Getting Customers*. S-Curves, 2014. Print.

Take Credit

Self-Promotion: Godin, Seth. *Self Promotion*. Seth's Blog. December 18, 2007. Web.

Be Consistent

Visiting every country: Guillebeau, Chris. *The Art of Non-Conformity.* Web. (**http://chrisguillebeau.com**)

Communicate Strength

Stay vigorous: Schultz, Howard, and Dori Jones. Yang. *Pour Your Heart into It: How Starbucks Built a Company One Cup at a Time.* New York, NY: Hyperion, 1997. Print.

Rest

Doing it: Gerber, Michael E. *The E-myth Revisited: Why Most Small Businesses Don't Work and What to Do about It.* New York: CollinsBusiness, 1995. Print.

ABOUT THE AUTHOR

Tara Gentile is a business strategist and the creator of Quiet Power Strategy™. She coaches business owners on how to find what's most effective for them so they can lead themselves to the results they crave. Tara transitioned from an academic pursuit of religion and theology to a holistic but analytical approach to business in the New Economy.

Her work has been featured in *Fast Company*, Forbes.com, DailyWorth, and Design*Sponge. She's a regular instructor for CreativeLive.

Find out more and download the Quiet Power Strategy™ Map at taragentile.com/quietpower.

ACKNOWLEDGEMENTS

I'd like to offer a special thanks to my mom, Rosanna Nevius, and my co-conspirator, Brigitte Lyons. I'm eternally grateful to my knight-in-shining-armor editor, Amy Scott of Nomad Editorial. My thanks goes to the friends who support me, push me, and help me rally: Megan Auman, Tanya Geisler, Megan Eckman, and Dr. Samantha Brody. More thanks goes to my CreativeLive producers who have challenged me to reach for new ways to communicate, create, and teach over the last year: Michael Karsh, Elizabeth Madariaga, and David Moldawer. Thank you to my cover designer, Tracey Selingo. And thank you to my amazing clients and community who have helped me to experiment with these ideas over the last 6 years.

Final thanks goes to my daughter, Lola, for being my inspiration to never settle for less than what I'm capable of and my partner, Sean, for always telling me how proud he is of me every day.

Made in the USA
San Bernardino, CA
14 February 2015